DON'T BET YOUR BARBIE® MONEY

AND 23 OTHER GREAT DON'T'S OF LIFE

NOTICES

DON'T BET YOUR BARBIE® MONEY

AND 23 OTHER GREAT DON'T'S OF LIFE

BEN GLASS
www.BenGlassLaw.com

DAN S. KENNEDY
www.DanKennedy.com

Published by: Kennedy Inner Circle, Inc.
15433 N. Tatum Blvd., #104, Phoenix, AZ 85032
Licensed for reprint to certain authorized additional publishers.

Authorized Publisher: BenGlassLaw/Great Legal Marketing
3915 Old Lee Highway
Suite 22-B
Fairfax, VA 22030

DISCLAIMER AND/OR LEGAL NOTICES:

Cover design: zinegraphics.com
Cover photo: istockphoto.com

PRINTED IN THE UNITED STATES OF AMERICA

Printed and Published by: Word Association Publishers
205 Fifth Avenue
Tarentum, Pennsylvania 15084
www.wordassociation.com
1.800.827.7903

HERE'S A COOL COUPON WORTH 2 TIMES WHAT YOU PAID FOR THIS BOOK!

Go to the Great Legal Marketing Webstore (GLMWebstore.com) and use the code "barbie50" to get $50.00 off any order $150.00 or above. Our thanks to you for reading this book.

ABOUT THE AUTHORS

BEN GLASS is a practicing attorney in Fairfax, VA. He has authored numerous consumer guides, including *The Five Deadly Sins That Can Wreck Your Injury Claim, Robbery Without a Gun,* and *Why Most Medical Malpractice Victims Never Recover a Dime.* Ben is a national authority on the subject of attorney marketing and has gained acclaim for applying marketing tactics from many other fields to the legal profession, even when others said it couldn't be done. His legal marketing company, Great Legal Marketing, coaches hundreds of attorneys across the nation, in addition to putting on a number of conferences that draw sold-out crowds every year. You can order the official Great Legal Marketing book at GreatLegalMarketingBook.com

Ben resides in Northern Virginia with his wife Sandi and together they have nine children (four of whom are adopted from China). Ben has run the Marine Corps Marathon 5 times on behalf of Love Without Boundaries, an organization dedicated to changing the lives of orphaned and impoverished children in China. He also serves on the board of Love Without Boundaries.

DAN KENNEDY is a multi-millionaire serial entrepreneur, celebrated author of numerous books published in the U.S. and abroad (in translated editions) and recognized by *INC.,* *ENTREPRENEUR, FORBES* and other leading publications, and a sought after consultant and direct marketing strategist. He is the editor of *THE NO B.S. MARKETING LETTER* and five other professional newsletters. As a speaker, he has repeatedly appeared on programs with leading business and success speakers including Zig Ziglar, Brian Tracy and Tom Hopkins, as well as numerous celebrity entrepreneurs including Gene Simmons (KISS), Donald Trump, Ivanka Trump, Debbi Fields (Mrs. Fields Cookies), George Foreman and Joan Rivers, as well as four former U.S. Presidents and other world leaders. The organization he originated and continues contributing to as content provider and advisor, Glazer-Kennedy Insider's Circle™, now literally spans the globe, directly serves about 25,000 members, additionally distributes business information through hundreds of thought-leaders in diverse industries, has local Chapters meeting in many cities, and conducts two major marketing-oriented conferences a year. Information about the author's books and activities may be accessed at **www.NoBSBooks.com**. Direct communication with the author should be done via fax: 602/269-3113. (E-mail to any of his publishers' web sites will not receive personal attention or response.) Mr. Kennedy is available for a very limited number of interesting and appropriate speaking, consulting, writing or direct-response copywriting engagements each year.

Mr. Kennedy lives in Ohio and Virginia, with his 2nd and 3rd wife (one and the same) and The Million Dollar Dog, although his office is in Arizona. He owns a stable of Standardbred racehorses and personally drives professionally in over 200 races a year, most at Northfield Park. Races can be seen at NorthfieldPark.com or on the cable TV network TVG.

CONTENTS

1 DON'T BET YOUR BARBIE™ MONEY. EVER.

(Dan)

Our daughter Jennifer told me of a childhood experience of hers that I had forgotten. Apparently, when she was young, I was teaching her how to play craps with a little tabletop craps game. (I never claimed to be "father of the year.") Anyway, at some point, she insisted on playing with real money instead of toy chips. "I had eighteen dollars saved up to buy a Barbie™, and I lost it all, and you wouldn't give it back," she recalled.

After a moment, I asked, "And what lesson did you learn from that?"

"Don't bet your Barbie™ money."

To this day, she doesn't gamble, and now I understand her aversion.

I am not opposed to gambling myself, and I often wager on horse races, bet pro football in season, and play blackjack casually if in a casino. I do not think gambling is evil or harmful, except for those who can't control their impulses and have compulsion/addiction issues. But then fast cars, sex, alcohol, fattening food, such odd behaviors as hoarding cats or trash (the subject of three reality TV shows, as I write this), and even cosmetic surgery pose just as much danger to individuals with certain addiction issues. That does not make sports cars or kittens or doughnuts *evil*. However, there are real lessons to be drawn from Jennifer's "defining moment" in my dining room casino. Here they are, as I know them:

Everybody needs to take risk and manage risk. You should not fear or avoid risk, nor should you carelessly, recklessly, or unnecessarily put yourself or your assets at risk. This is a tightrope every entrepreneur defines for himself or herself and walks daily. Specific to money, only a percentage should be put at high risk for great possible gain, a percentage at some risk for moderate gain, and a percentage at zero risk. You should always pay yourself first, with a percentage of every dollar diverted into "untouchables" as you go. For more about converting income to wealth, I refer you to the discussion of wealth and giving accounts in my book, *NO B.S. WEALTH*

> **EVERYBODY NEEDS TO TAKE RISK AND MANAGE RISK.**

ATTRACTION IN THE NEW ECONOMY, available at all bookstores and online booksellers.

By the way, for those thinking, "mean Daddy who wouldn't give the little nine-year-old girl her money back," you might as well know I'm pretty consistent about this. I don't believe in sheltering anybody from reality, in making kids weak and fragile by preventing them from eating dirt, getting a tooth knocked out playing dodge ball, or receiving a failing grade. I don't give or accept excuses for poor performance. Of course, what you choose to do with your kids is your business. I claim no special expertise in parenting. I would say that there's reason we see so many thumb-sucking twenty-year-olds moving back in with mommy and daddy these days, but still not my point. My main point is about how you parent *you.*

Having a thought-out, organized philosophy of self-management is just as rare as is exceptional success, not coincidentally. You might think of this as a navigational system, maps, and GPS. Or a system of governance, like the Constitution. How you operate you. Within, the question: Do you or do you not accept excuses for inferior performance? Do you or do you not easily let yourself off the hook? My *RENEGADE MILLIONAIRE SYSTEM* is largely about the development of your own, formal navigational system. Don't wander around out there without one.

DON'T SETTLE FOR LESS

(Dan)

I would like to encourage you to get rich – or, if you are already rich, to get richer. The economy needs your wealth, because your subtractions equal addition and even multiplication for the economy. We urgently need more rich people. Even more urgently, we need more people in "full court press," acting on their ambition to get rich. If you understand this concept, then you will stop settling for less than you really want.

I would like to encourage you to value whatever you know and do and sell much more than you do. The proper installation of a tire on a car seems a small thing, and most mechanics think of it in mundane terms – whatever they make as hourly wage, divided by minutes required to mount the tire. But if you've ever had an improperly installed tire come off at 40 or 50 miles an hour, you have a different view of the value of that job done right, done reliably, by an expert and entirely trustworthy person. Of course, conveying that higher value to consumers in a cluttered, competitive marketplace isn't easy, and left sold and priced as that job rather than re-configured into a guaranteed personal auto safety and maintenance program sold by membership, by month or year, it is under severe price pressure. I acknowledge that reality, but I also assure you, it is possible to create your own reality and bring more than enough other people into it, to support you in grand style, with what you do valued high—not low. You need this how-to knowledge, so you can be paid what you genuinely deserve.

As I write this book, I am personally paid $18,800 to sit with a private business client for 6 hours, to be asked questions about marketing and to answer them to the best of my ability. I am paid upwards from $100,000 plus royalties to develop marketing systems and materials and write advertising copy for such a client. What I do isn't as commonplace as, say, mounting tires on cars – done at most tire shops and service stations. But it is still commonplace. There are lots of marketing consultants who will happily sit and dispense their advice for a lot less than $18,800 a day – and many aggressively advertise and promote themselves, so they're not a secret. There are lots of copywriters who will write ad campaigns for less than $100,000 – and many aggressively advertise and promote themselves, so they're not a secret. We each decide what we are worth. Many people think the marketplace makes that determination. That false idea is even taught at all the prestigious business schools, so Ph.D.s believe it as religion. It is only true if it is your reality. Or you

6

can choose my reality, where the marketplace does NOT determine your worth or your price; you do.

I think your ability to make a lot of money, all the money you want and a bit more, and to make it without trading away

WE EACH DECIDE WHAT WE ARE WORTH.

your every waking moment for forty or fifty or sixty years—or selling your soul—is enormously important.

It's a bad idea to underestimate the importance of money. The anti-money clichés, like "money can't buy happiness," are extremely popular with people who have little money and little willingness to exert the effort required for wealth, or even a good income. But they are merely parroting the clichés, not speaking from personal experience. It so happens that I have personally been poor, been broke, been frightened and pained and humiliated and desperate because of it, and I have created high income, and I have gotten rich, so I can speak on this subject from personal experience. And I will tell you: money can, in fact, buy happiness. Of course, happiness is a subjective thing. But owning my horses makes me happy. The fact that I own them, that I have the ability to stop by and visit them, that I actually drive them in races makes me happy – and costs a helluva lot of money. Living in a nice, paid-for home; driving a good, reliable car absent bald tires or duct tape; having clothes tailored to fit; by-passing the airlines and flying by private jet; not having to tell myself or my wife "we can't afford it" – these things make me happy and require money. Sure, the sunny day is free to all, and with no money in your pocket, it is possible to be happy, because you are alive and taking a nice walk on a sunny day. But money worries can certainly spoil such a day. And driving down a country road in my Rolls-Royce convertible on a sunny day makes me happier than standing at a bus stop, waiting for a bus on that same sunny day.

Money buys a lot of relatively intangible, non-material benefits and privileges, not just objects and things. It buys a sense of security and peace of mind, freedom and liberty, autonomy and independence, self-confidence, opportunity to influence others, and the capability of aiding others in need or with worthy pursuits. Sure, you can stand on a soapbox purloined from behind a grocer's store, speak to passers-by, and possibly be influential. It's often pointed out to me that Jesus ran a low-budget operation. I say: that was then, this is now. It takes over a billion dollars to run for president. The Salvation Army needs an awful lot of money to feed the hungry and minister to souls – based on the amount of mail I get from them, they need A LOT. Sure, ultimately, peace of mind is a state of mind; your thoughts are your own, and they are free. But see how many people you can find who live paycheck to paycheck, have never learned to create high-value marketable skills or profitable enterprises, and worry over the drawer of bills--yet have peace of mind.

Not only shouldn't you under-value money, you shouldn't settle for any less of it—and all it will buy, including the opportunity to arrange your entire life as you would like it to be – **than you really want**. I was fortunately made to understand: abundance is an ocean that does not care if you come to it with spoon, bucket, or tanker truck. It is endlessly accommodating of all requests – and surprised and disappointed by how little so many ask of it. If you doubt its existence and feel inhibited, timid, or guilty about taking more than your fair share or taking too much—or that your taking bars others from having—then you must get and read my book *NO B.S. WEALTH ATTRACTION IN THE NEW ECONOMY,* available at all bookstores and online booksellers. You NEED to read it. It will dis-abuse you of your incorrect ideas about prosperity and equip you with the true principles. If you are anxious or timid about asserting yourself and requiring the entire world to bow to your will and let you live the life you really want, you need to get and read my *NO B.S. TIME MANAGEMENT FOR ENTREPRENEURS* and my *NO B.S. RUTHLESS MANAGEMENT OF PEOPLE AND PROFITS* books. If you are weak when selling yourself, your goods, your services at your desired prices, get the *NO B.S. SALES SUCCESS IN THE NEW ECONOMY* and *NO B.S. PRICE STRATEGY* books.

"It is better to have a permanent income than to be fascinating."

– Oscar Wilde

3 DON'T FRET YESTERDAY

(Ben)

There was a time when I tried to take up golf. I know – hard to believe. When does a guy with nine kids play golf? It was a long time ago, 1995, in fact. I had just started my own practice. I had four kids and a dog. ("The perfect size family," Sandi and I thought.) I had a ton of free time in my practice – not, mind you, because everything ran perfectly on systems – but because I had very few cases! We used to take a half day off on Fridays, and on Thursday mornings I took golf lessons. On other mornings, I went out and "played" (using that term *very* loosely) at dawn. By myself. Life was good, but the golf game wasn't.

I never was very good, but the one thing I really liked about golf was that at each hole I started back at ZERO strokes. No matter how many shots taken (or balls lost in woods, tall grass, and water) on the previous hole, I started at ZERO on the next hole. A fresh start. I was pretty good at getting the last hole out of my head.

The reason I bring this up is that the last few years were really lousy for a lot of people. Lawyers and small business owners alike. You almost couldn't avoid the financial mess. For some, major disasters. For some, maybe just more paperwork to get credit or buy a house. On some days I wondered, "What the heck is going on here?" I've talked to many lawyers and small biz owners who actually gave up and quit. One thing I've gotten pretty good at is starting each day as a brand-new opportunity. A gift, really. Like heading to the 9th hole after shooting a twelve on 8, we get to start over and begin again. What happened in the past does not direct what happens going forward. Block it out – learn from whatever mistake or choice you made – move on. If you are going to scream and shout at the world, limit yourself to an hour.

Now, more than ever, you need to invest in yourself. It's not going to be the stock market that provides financial security (unless you are running for congress, apparently). Not from what I can

> **WHAT HAPPENED IN THE PAST DOES NOT DIRECT WHAT HAPPENS GOING FORWARD.**

see. It's going to be you and your business and your continued ability to differentiate yourself in a very crowded market.

What I've been doing over the winter break is spending a lot of time investing in myself. First, seeing a good rehab specialist for a nagging calf injury from my last marathon. I hate not being able to run. I hate even more having to do stretching and PT and all that stuff every day, but I want to be able to keep running for a long time. Next, I've spent time looking at my marketing assets. We've got over 400 videos. You know what? Some of them "seemed like a good idea at the time," but in reality they are not very good. What good ones do we have? Where could my website be improved? What articles written years ago to market my law practice can be turned into new articles or videos? I've also been investing in other people's products. Right now, I'm watching a 14-disk DVD set on "Marketing Your Book." Sure, lots of it I already know, but I've already picked up one BIG tip on free publicity that I wasn't using. I also spent two days over the break assembling one of those portable basketball goals. When you've got kids who are 28 and others who are 9, you get to do stuff like assemble "fairly complex and heavy" basketball goals twice in one lifetime!

My question for you is: what are you doing right now to re-start, to pick yourself up if your last year wasn't great? You have to ask yourself this question every single day: what do I know today that I didn't know about my business yesterday? If the answer is "nothing," look again.

DON'T TELL THE TRUTH, & DON'T EASILY ACCEPT THE TRUTH TOLD BY OTHERS

(Dan)

Truth telling is a vastly over-rated, over-hyped virtue.

For example, I am leaving my house to go to an important meeting, in suit, shirt, and tie, running late. My first ex-wife would regularly ask: "You aren't going to wear *that* tie with *that* suit, are you?" Notice the sentence construction. She didn't ask, "Are you going to wear that tie with that suit?" No. She asked in a way that told me what the correct answer was supposed to be. This is pretty useful if you pay attention. The correct answer here would be: "No, I hadn't decided yet. Just trying it out. Do you have a better one to suggest, Dear?"

The correct answer is *not*, "No, you moron, I just put it on for practice and headed out the door to see what the neighbors thought of it. YES, I'm wearing this tie with this suit."

Also notice: first ex-wife. Two strikes, three balls, full count, batter up.

There are clearly all sorts of situations where it is smart, if not vitally necessary, to lie. For "thou shalt not lie" to work, God would have had to install truth-welcoming receptors in human brains. If that was the intent, the work coming off the assembly line for planet earth has been defective since the start.

There's often the option of saying nothing at all. But to quote comedian Ron White, "I know I had the *right* to remain silent. I just didn't have the *ability*."

> THERE ARE CLEARLY ALL SORTS OF SITUATIONS WHERE IT IS SMART... TO LIE.

Anyway, back to the question and answer dance. This is a valuable business, persuasion and communication tool kit, the structure of questions and answers and sentences. You can structure questions in a way that assists the other person in seeing things your way, agreeing with you, or accepting your proposition. Most people are unsure of themselves, so they actually welcome sign that point them in the right direction. Question prefaces like "as I'm sure you know," or "as you probably know," or "I'm sure you'll agree" are used in selling for the express purpose of controlling the answer. Or a benefit-affirming question like, "I'll bet nobody you've ever done business with in your entire life has offered you such a strong guarantee, right?" Or a question much like the tie question: "You wouldn't want your family to miss out on an experience like this, would you?" clearly telegraphs the correct answer. If the family happens to be sitting there when it's asked, you can sometimes see little beads of sweat appear on the poor fellow's forehead.

But even more valuable than the careful construction of the questions you ask, is the careful listening to the questions others ask of you. By being conscious about this, you can spot and escape traps. "You're absolutely right, I want my family to have the best of everything – but, at the moment, I am most concerned with meeting our savings goals for the three boys' college educations, so I'm going to have to give a firm and final no to your offer – and I'm sure my wife agrees with me, right, Dear?" You can see what the person asking you a question hopes to receive as the answer and choose whether or not to provide it. You can answer a question with a question, thereby actually controlling the conversation. You can even stay married.

Here's a not-so-little secret: successful sales professionals and others engaged in persuasion, leaders, influencers, and entrepreneurs are all *very conscious* of their communication. Thoughtful and deliberate, not casual. Strategic, not random. Practiced, not spontaneous. They are serious students of the art and science of influence. They are interested in stimulus-response, whether in advertising or conversation, in the boardroom or in the kitchen. I can recommend some authors whose works you might include in your own serious study: Dr. Frank

Luntz, Dr. Cialdini, Paco Underhill, to name few of many. They also tend to go to considerable trouble to stage and control the environment in which they communicate. The president of the United States does not deliver a speech to the American public via his cell-phone while standing at men's room urinal or driving down the expressway, munching on a burrito from the Taco Bell drive-in. He delivers speeches in very controlled environments, well prepared, perfectly attired, backdrop chosen; he free of distractions, able to concentrate, conscious of facial expression and voice inflection. Of course, your telephone conversation with a client or your sit-down with a customer at your shop probably isn't as important as is an explanation of war or a selling of a billion dollar plan by the president. It might be *more* important to you.

The other interesting thing about a lot of truth is that it is subjective, but fiercely defended. Consider the existence of God. And I have just ventured into dangerous territory, haven't I? Believers know that God is fact. His existence is truth and anyone asserting otherwise is ignorant or evil or a liar. In truth, there is no actual certain knowledge to what they devoutly believe. Their truth is belief. Non-believers divide into agnostics and atheists. Agnostics acknowledge the *possibility* of God as any number of possible explanations for the little globe we're all parked on but do not subscribe to any belief system built around the existence of God. Their truth is, essentially, who knows? Atheists insist that their truth is science, but there is no scientific proof ruling out the possibility of God. Each of these people owns a separate and different truth. None can irrefutably evidence their truth. Gravity on earth is a *more* objective truth, yet we have been able to make it malleable with inventions like the hot air balloon, blimp, airplane, helicopter, jet pack, and, depending on how much you believe what your eyes see, magicians' levitation. But truth about God is very subjective. If you operated by the principle of always speaking only the truth, the *absolute* truth, if Christian, you could not speak of the existence of God as anything but hopeful opinion – yet you do and will never accept the proposition that you are a liar. If atheist, the same goes for your assertions that there is no God, yet you consider yourself the only truth-teller surrounded by mystics and charlatans. This truth thing is tricky. Some lying can be exposed as lying, but it's not so simple to tell the truth.

And what of the person who tells himself he can do something that he has never done or even that no one has ever done and sets out on a quest to do it – perhaps mortgaging his family's home and endangering their financial security to bring his invention to market or leading the American revolution against the British, putting everybody's necks at risk? Does he lie to himself or others when he speaks the confident certainty and reassurance required to inspire their investment and allegiance? What of the coach who gathers his young men in the locker room at half time, trailing an opponent by two touchdowns – an opponent that objective assessment says is bigger, stronger, faster, more skilled, and that expert oddsmakers have favored by four touchdowns – and he convinces them that they can return to the battle, make up the deficit, and win this contest, thus putting them at risk of severe disappointment, endangering their self-esteem, and almost certainly lying to them based on what he actually believes to be the truth of the situation? Should this coach instead speak the truth as he knows it? On the occasions when such locker room pep talks do fire up an over-matched underdog team, and they do go out and "win one for the Gipper," what was the truth?

In his book *The Success System That Never Fails,* self-made billionaire W. Clement Stone tells of saving a struggling sales-man, going down for the third time, by giving him a list of names of well-chosen prospective buyers for life insurance, prospects represented by Stone as exceptionally well-quali-fied, and virtually certain to be receptive. He even went so far as to encourage the floundering salesman to "feel free to use my name" when contacting the prospects. In truth, Stone had hastily chosen names of business executives at random from a directory and scribbled them on a slip of paper. They did not know Stone and Stone did not know them. The list was a lie. But also a placebo with power over the attitude and actions of the salesman. And so, what kind of a lie was it? And, since the punch line of the story is that several of the prospects on that slip of paper did, in fact, prove receptive and met with the agent and purchased insurance from him, was it a lie at all? Or a lie with a truth inside? Was W. Clement Stone a liar or a revealer of truth – truth both about the marketplace for insurance and about this salesman?

I came up in multi-level/network marketing, a business cen-tered around taking ordinary people and turning them into extraordinary salespeople and motivational leaders, something akin to turning gerbils into circus acrobats. I have personally seen painfully shy and timid people, frightened of life itself, about whom a life's truth was that they could not sell and would never dare try selling let alone stand on a stage before hundreds or thousands with microphone in hand and confidently, persuasively deliver an inspiring speech producing a standing ovation metamorphose into exactly such dynamic salespeople and speakers – thus altering truth itself.

The really odd thing about truth is that, while past is predictive prologue for most people, it is *not* for *all* people and therefore need *not* be for *any* person, so whatever the truth about you has been to this point – whether you're seventeen or seventy-seven – it does not need to be the truth today or tomorrow. None need be who they are, stay where they are, act as they now act. One of the classic books in the world of selling, by Frank Bettger, is titled *How I Raised Myself from Failure to Success in Selling*. Its title is the story of countless men and women who raise themselves from one reality to an entirely different reality of their own choosing. Such replacement of one set of truths with another set is statistically rare yet still quite common.

Many speak what they believe to be absolute truth – and in doing so, lie. *Peanuts'* creator Schultz fired from Disney for having no talent as a cartoonist. *Chicken Soup for the Soul* rejected by hundreds of experienced editors at successful publishing houses, as having no marketability and seeming a naïve and foolish idea. A friend of mine, four-time Super Bowl champion Rocky Bleier, was told he was way too small for pro football, and after injuries, before getting those rings, told he could not return to the game. Opinion is endlessly put forward as absolute truth and all too often accepted as truth by those to whom it is directed, when it is nothing but opinion. Actual truth has some inherent power. Opinion has power only when accepted as truth. Its power must be gifted to it by those it seeks to control. You want to remember that whenever opinion seeks to control you.

OPINION HAS POWER ONLY WHEN ACCEPTED AS TRUTH

5 DON'T DISQUALIFY YOURSELF

(Dan)

You're never too young. The kid who birthed Facebook made himself a billionaire before age thirty. He's a dramatic example, but far from a rare one. Lots of kids create hugely profitable enterprises, even part-time, while attending school. If you're ever passing through Dayton, Ohio, check out Grunder Landscaping. Big company. Marty, now a millionaire, started it with one lawn mower and sweat, while going to school.

You're never too old. Check out the biography of Colonel Sanders. At Northfield Park, the racetrack where I drive professionally most of the time, there are very capable, competitive drivers winning in a young man's game. John Green, age seventy-three. Eldon Spearman, age eighty-two.

DON'T BET YOUR BARBIE® MONEY

You're never too poor. A client of mine, for whom I wrote advertising, started her little business with nothing more than a bucket, a mop, and a one-page photocopied flier, after the restaurant she owned with her husband went bankrupt. She built a million-dollar cleaning business, sold it, retired, wrote a "how-to" course to teach others how to start such businesses – and sold thousands of those. A good friend, the late Dottie Walters, made sales calls for her first business with her baby along in the stroller because she couldn't afford a babysitter, and from that start, built the largest welcome-new-move-in advertising company in southern California.

You're never too dumb. Check out the lack of higher education on the *Forbes* list of richest people, published each year. For the record, I have a high school education and no more. Every professional skill I've developed to a high level is self-taught. I am routinely paid upwards of $100,000 to write advertising. I attended no college, took no course, served no apprenticeship, and never held a job in advertising in an agency or any other company's employ. Years back, I worked on production of a TV infomercial having to do with illiteracy, hosted by the actor Danny Glover. In interviewing the many testimonials for the course being sold, I met a man who had built a home services business to over five million dollars a year in sales before he ever learned to read. His wife kept the books and wrote the checks. He did everything else 'in his head." Having reached age forty-two without ever learning to read, he'd been too ashamed to let anybody know and, as he put it, too busy gettin' rich to fix it. He said: "I found out I could hire readers kinda cheap."

No, I don't recommend illiteracy. Quite the contrary. But he stands testament to the fact that education and achievement and wealth are not necessarily linked. Today, by the way, there's zero excuse to stay ignorant about any information needed to pursue any goal. If you can type its name into Google, you can start getting smarter.

You're never done. Iacocca was fired by Ford. Jack Welch, one of today's most admired business thinkers and leaders, left his top dog spot at GE and a marriage rather hastily, under cloud of an embarrassing little sex scandal with a journalist. I've gone through bankruptcy.

YOU'RE NEVER DONE.

You're never "out of your league." Donald Trump's father bought and renovated small houses in low to middle class neighborhoods, and thought his son's gigantic ambitions fantastical. Oprah struggled early on as a local market talk show host, and as she begun her climb nationally, there was no good reason to believe a large, brash *black woman* could supplant an entire array of more experienced, polished, popular daytime talk hosts. Kurt Warner was rebuffed by all NFL teams, bagging groceries, and playing in the Arena League when he got his NFL opportunity due to a starting quarterback's injuries. I was one of only two speakers on the #1 seminar tour in America, appearing in twenty-five to twenty-seven cities a year for nine years, to audiences as large as 10,000 to 35,000, with former

U.S. presidents, world leaders, *Fortune* 1000 CEOs, legendary entrepreneurs, and sports and Hollywood celebrities, as well as the four top speakers of this time: Zig Ziglar, Brian Tracy, Tom Hopkins, and Jim Rohn. I possess none of the National Speakers Association's credentials like "certified speaking professional." I had a severe stutter as a child.

You're never too "anything." Too busy? John Grisham wrote his first legal thriller while commuting on the subway. He is a multi-millionaire, enormously successful writer of popular novels, several turned into movies. Too odd? My friend Mark Victor Hansen's *Chicken Soup for the Soul* book series was summarily rejected by hundreds of publishers. Too small? Ask Fran Tarkenton. Too ugly? That's what movie studios said of Burt Reynolds and Clint Eastwood. Too "damaged"? Refer to Chapter 10. Too weak? Research the life story of Charles Atlas.

If there's a STOP sign in the middle of your driveway, you put it there. You are free to remove it any time you like.

DON'T LET YOUR COMPETITION CATCH YOU

(Ben)

I had an interesting conversation with my son David recently. David is fifteen. In January we marked the anniversary of "family day." That's the day when we met David and Leah (fourteen) in Beijing, China. (Yes, we were in Beijing a few winters ago, just as Chinese New Year was starting. You haven't seen anything 'til you've seen Chinese New Year!)

Anyway… David has been reading the biography of Steve Jobs. Although his English is very, very good, now, he's been reading the Chinese version. He's also been listening to the audio version in English. This morning, David said, "Steve Jobs reveals a lot about Apple…how they thought about things… how they came up with ideas…. how they created the special glass that is used in iPads and iPhones… how they hired and fired."

Then David asked, "Isn't he afraid that people will steal his secrets and use them? Why does he reveal so much?"

I told him that Jobs knew what I know: you can show people *everything* and most are just too lazy to keep up with you. David knows about my marketing and he knows that I show every-thing—knowing that most will just never get around to doing what my team and I are doing.

MOST ARE JUST TOO LAZY TO KEEP UP WITH YOU.

I run an "Attorney MasterMind Group" where we share all our secrets. Each meeting is two days of "I saw what you did last meeting three months ago and now let me show you how I improved on it." After a day that started at 8:00 a.m. and finished with a group dinner at 9:00, I was up at 3:00 a.m. in my hotel room, working with my InfusionSoft program based on ONE LITTLE THING I heard another member say. The morning after I landed back here in Virginia, I was up at 5:00 a.m. to re-work my YouTube videos based on ONE LITTLE THING that one of our members revealed at the VERY END OF OUR MEETING. (He had heard the idea at another MasterMind meeting he had been in on the other side of the country with some of the world's top Internet marketers, just days before our meeting took place. My MasterMind mem-bers are amazing!)

I ended by telling David that there are two things that will make him successful: (1) always be a learner and (2) work harder than anyone else. As I walked him to the bus stop, he told me that he was staying after school to go to the running club meeting so that he'll be ready for the high school cross country team *in a year and a half.*

What have you done today to make sure that your competition can't touch you?

7 DON'T WAIT

(Dan)

So much misery, unhappiness, fecklessness, poverty, unused potential, and wasted opportunity is product purely and simply of *waiting*.

Not procrastinating – that's a different evil.

Of waiting. Many, for example, *wait for others' permission* to do things. In every occupational pursuit I've ever succeeded wildly at – including professional speaking, advertising copywriting, writing – I was set upon by some group of wise elders and official authorities telling me I had to grovel before crawling, crawl before walking, walk before running, take whatever table scraps offered before bellying up to the big people's buffet. They have their own fear and envy based reasons for pushing this horseshit on people. I have ignored it all, and, to use my friend Robert Ringer's term, "leap-frogged." Ladders are for others.

Many people wait for good timing, whatever that is. I've been in business for myself, creating my own opportunities, income, and wealth for about thirty-six or thirty-seven years at this writing. I've yet to see the unicorn of good timing. Sure, there have been national economies more generous than grumpy and more grumpy than generous at different times. I began my business career in earnest during the Jimmy Carter recession and there were strong headwinds. My success had helpful winds at its back during the Reagan revival of the economy. But there's more to timing than the national economy. There's always some

I'VE YET TO SEE THE UNICORN OF GOOD TIMING.

personal reason or financial reason or reason seemingly unique to your niche to wait. People who live sequentially are always waiting for some next reason to wait to erase itself, waiting to get more established at work before advancing new initiatives, to get bills paid down before saving and investing, to get the kids through school before re-locating or launching a business. There's always a good-sounding reason to wait. Even as one reason is dissipating, another materializes.

Most people wait endlessly about most things for a dizzy-ing variety of reasons. And most ultimately regret the actions endlessly postponed, the roads never traveled, the words not said far, far, far more than whatever is done.

We are, I suppose, conditioned to wait. We begin life waiting for our parents to feed us, clothe us, pick us up, move us. I didn't; I twice rocked my crib entirely out of my room, across a second floor living area, and sent it crashing down the steps in struggle to get to where the action was. But most of the in-the-crib age spend a whole lot of time waiting. Wailing too, but still, waiting. In youth, we wait for permission and often get into serious trouble if we act without it. We are taught to raise our hands in class and wait – even when we need to go to the bathroom. We wait in lines, it seems, for damn near everything, although smart people can and do find ways to circumvent a lot of lines. At Disney, you can hire a private guide and never stand in a line. I can give my assistant a note on which I've written what I want to buy – a book, a gift, a pair of cowboy boots – and I never need to stand in a line to get to a cash register. I fly now by private jet, so I never stand in lines at airports. You can too. These things only require money and there's an endless supply of that. But most people wait in lots and lots and lots of lines. They even camp out over night and stand in line to be let into stores to be among the first to buy the latest gadget. At the movie theater, people wait in line to buy a ticket, then wait in line to get past the ticket-taking kid, then wait in line at the refreshment counter to pay eight dollars for a soft drink, then sit and wait to watch commercials before finally seeing the movie. I find this a thoroughly disagreeable experience, but a lot of people are just fine with it. Many businesses have places that are actually called "waiting rooms" and people go, even with pre-set appointments they are required to make, knowing they will have to arrive at the time agreed, but then sit for who-knows-how-long in a waiting room. That people have been convinced *this* is acceptable is testament to the power of all this conditioning from birth.

This kind of waiting mind-set carries over to *everything*. Since most people have been conditioned, brainwashed, trained, intimidated into waiting; believe waiting is normal and customary and unavoidable; and expect to wait, that's what they do: wait. They wait for the cable guy as if he is Godot. So, they wait to start a business, launch a product, fire a toxic employee, confront a difficult client, tackle a brewing problem, etc., etc., etc. The vast majority are waiting. Waiting to see what will happen. Waiting for somebody else to solve a problem. Waiting for the weather or the economy to change, their ill-behaved child to grow out of it, the busy season to pass before they tackle x, y, or z. There is a bad, old joke: a couple, both obviously quite elderly, appear before the magistrate at divorce court. He asks how long they've been married and is told "forty-three years." He kindly, curiously inquires why, after all this time, at their advanced ages, they're now getting divorced. They answer: "We've been waiting for the kids to die."

PATIENCE, LIKE TRUTH, IS A GROSSLY OVER-RATED VIRTUE.

Here is quite possibly the biggest single secret of exceptionally successful people: *they start*. They start things. They start *without* sufficient resources, *without* enough time, *without* the money, heck, *without* knowing what they are doing! They start before they are ready. They start without concern for being ready. They start. At times they are, by normal standards – and that's an important phrase – reckless, foolhardy, over-committed, ill equipped, unreasonable.

Walt began Disneyland far short of the resources or know-how needed to pull it off and absent any idea of where or how all the necessary capital and other resources might be pulled together. He famously cut a last-minute deal with ABC to get the money needed to open the gates. Lacking the money to finish landscaping, he made up Latin sounding names of fictional plants, had them written on signs and stuck in front of weeds. Had he not started this way, odds are great he would never have gotten started. The grand opening of Disneyland was not all that grand, and it was panned and criticized in the media. For about five years, as a speaker, I followed General Norman Schwarzkopf, a great leader, on about twenty programs a year. Norm said that it was a lot easier to fix something started than to start, easier to re-direct something on a better course than to accomplish anything waiting and never starting. That's what Walt did. He started, then he fixed.

This is not to say you should be *unnecessarily* reckless, and I am certainly not championing *unnecessary* ignorance. But if you require perfect timing, absence of obstacles, all knowns and no unknowns, permission from others, sunny skies, dry roads, and a GPS before starting, you are forever stopped. You may think of it as waiting, but it's very probably permanent.

This book has probably reached you because you are a business owner or entrepreneur or self-employed professional or a creative person like a writer or artist, which means you possess talent or at least skill, know-how, probably ambition, and opportunity. It could very well be true that you are also, at this very moment, waiting to finalize some pending decisions, act on some pregnant opportunity, make some significant change, act on some ambition or idea – and waiting for what? Almost no one ever achieves anything by waiting. And it is rarer than most think that people avoid danger or pain or loss by waiting. More often, all they do is postpone it, worsen it, or have to hunt them down in their hiding place.

ALMOST NO ONE EVER ACHIEVES ANYTHING BY WAITING.

To be self-serving, I'll even narrow it to a question of waiting over some investment you might make with me or with some expert who passed along this book – perhaps attending an expensive seminar, joining a coaching program, buying a course. Let's assume we're talking about ten thousand dollars. That is, for the record, twenty-seven dollars a day if divided over a single year or two dollars and seventy cents a day if bearing fruit over ten years. If you earn a hundred thousand dollars a year over thirty years, it is .33%, i.e. one third of one percent of your earnings – thus it would need to boost your earnings by only two thirds of one percent to return double your investment. Maybe more significant, what will be gained by waiting to make this investment? And what will be lost? If you wait a year or two or three, that's a year or two or three during which no fruit can be harvested from the information or assistance, and mistakes bearing cost that might have been avoided with the information and assistance occur. The gain will be keeping the ten thousand dollars in your pocket, but, really, will it stay put in your pocket? The only real outcome from waiting to invest in self-improvement, skill improvement, or business improvement is delay. No gain is even *possible*. Worse, and maybe most important, by not starting, you are stopped.

Starting or waiting are two behavioral choices that tend to be habitual and even governing. Most people prone to waiting never start much, thus never go anywhere. Most people prone to starting rarely wait, thus getting a lot of places. Some of those places turn out to be bumpy rides, dead-ends or even crash landings off cliffs that bruise and injure, but other places turn out to be very fine indeed. Few get only to the latter places, and waiting to go anywhere definitely does not get you to the fine places. It just gets you where you are.

DON'T RUN AWAY FROM CONSUMER RATING SITES

(Ben)

Huge article in the *Washington Post* recently about doctors getting patients to sign "do not rate me or post anything negative about me online" forms BEFORE treatment begins. The article focused on the so-called "rights" of doctors to demand compliance and the "rights" of patients not to have to sign them. (There are no such "rights." Last I heard, the doctor-patient relationship is still a voluntary contract in America… but I digress.)

A Dallas law firm filed a lawsuit against "John Doe" because Johnny posted a negative review online. The firm wants to subpoena Google so they can track down John Doe. I guess they want to go tattle to his mommy.

Two thoughts immediately come to mind: (1) Trying to "go after" folks who write bad reviews about you has to be a time-wasting game of "whack-a-mole." Folks, there are more of them than there are of us. There's got to be a better way. (2) I would love to be the marketing director for a doctor marketing *against* someone forcing patients to sign those forms. My headline would be:

> **Do you really want to go to a doctor who is so unsure of the quality of her treatment that she forces you to sign a non-disclosure agreement before she takes your temperature for the first time?**

Look, effective use of the Internet is the fastest and most efficient lead generation tool for lawyers ever invented, so important to my practice that I am continually expanding my "Internet Marketing Domination Team." That being so, we can never let ourselves be in the position of arguing that we don't like certain parts of it, e.g., lawyer rating sites.

Embrace them. Figure out how to get more people to go there and "rate" you. In my office, EVERYONE we talk to gets a cool card that encourages him or her to go to TalkAboutBen.com and make a comment. (Go look at it.) There is no better "defense" against a negative comment here and there than a ton of positive comments. And…in a weird sort of way, the negative comments "validate" the good ones. I've shown my Great Legal Marketing/ MasterMind group our new program for getting LOTS of new Google reviews. All legit. All white hat. All real. In short, we do everything we can to continually ensure that anyone searching for a lawyer on the Internet will stumble upon us, find us interesting, and start the journey toward becoming "a member of the BenGlassLaw family."

DON'T ACCEPT THE FIRST "NO"

(Dan)

My third wife is my second wife.

I hold a professional harness racing driver's license that enables me to race over two hundred times a year, competing with top drivers – a license I had summarily revoked the first two times I obtained it, through arduous qualifying efforts. I was told nobody gets a third chance.

My first book manuscripts were rejected by a number of publishers and agents. I went to a publishers' convention and essentially door-knocked, got the ear of a publisher, dragged her by the ear to a meeting, and made a deal. I have since had more than twenty-five books published by five different publishers, and sixteen are currently available in bookstores and at online booksellers. My books have graced the *Business Week Magazine* and Amazon bestseller and *Inc. Magazine 100 Best Business Books* lists, hundreds of thousands of copies have been sold, and authorship of these books has made significant contribution to my prominence and wealth.

The kind of business I built from scratch, drew a seven-figure personal income from, made myself famous with, and twice sold – that ultimately evolved into the present Glazer-Kennedy Insider's Circle™ empire – had, as its predecessors two failed attempts, producing both a corporate and personal bankruptcy.

These are just a few of the biggest "no"s. I've heard "no" a whole lot, from a whole lot of different people, in nearly every state of the union, with varying degrees of ferocity.

My favorite "no" to "no" story is Kenneth Cole's. In short, he could not afford to exhibit in the exhibit halls of New York City's Fashion Week, so he ingeniously decided simply to rent a big truck or motor home, put his displays in it, park on the street near the convention center, and inveigle the fashion industry buyers and retailers to tour his exhibit. Of course, the City of New York's permit-issuing bureaucrats informed him he was insane. No one, repeat, *no one* can park a motor home or truck on a busy New York street for days on end. Cole did not believe them! Persisting, he uncovered the exception to the rule: movies. Quite a few movies have scenes filmed in the city, and their equipment trucks and actors' dressing rooms on wheels are routinely issued permits. So, "Kenneth Cole Productions" was born. When you see a Kenneth Cole billboard, magazine ad, store, shoes, or apparel in department stores, and consider the jobs created, business opportunities provided and taxes paid, know it all owes debt to the founder's refusal to take the first "no" as his answer.

This is the same basic story behind the story of so many of our greatest companies, as well as tens of thousands of successful small businesses, of invented products now in use in your home and business, of fortunes past and present, even of literary works and cultural achievements.

In selling, of course, it is axiomatic that the sale often begins when the customer says "no." That's basi-

THE SALE OFTEN BEGINS WHEN THE CUSTOMER SAYS "NO."

cally the difference between a consumer buying something, like a product from a shelf, and a consumer being sold something: the involvement of a salesperson unfazed by initial disinterest, skepticism, objection, or refusal. With the kind of marketing and preparation strategies I teach, to occur in advance of the involvement of the salesperson, much of this resistance can be erased or mitigated by various means – such as strategic, magnetic attraction of pre-interested, motivated, better qualified prospects who welcome the salesperson, or better advance preparation of the prospect. But these strategies themselves incorporate a dogged persistence, done via media rather than manual labor. You can see it spelled out in my book *NO B.S. SALES SUCCESS IN THE NEW ECONOMY,* available at all booksellers – specifically with the process begun in Chapter 18, beginning with "permission to sell." Attempting sex without permission is rape. Attempting selling without permission isn't criminally prosecutable, but it is criminally stupid.

Anyway, the combined attraction-marketing- -selling process is all about ignoring the first "no"s. In a pre-appointment marketing sequence integrating offline media, like sales letters and other direct-mail, and online media, like e-mail, we may have from three to thirty steps before surrender. Often, there will be what I call an "appointment, no sale" follow-up sequence too, first presenting the same offer, then modifying that offer, then switching to a different offer, sometimes of lower price or even alternate product or service, and such "systems" can bring from five to twenty percent of those who said "no" at the appointment back to the table and back to buy.

There are far too many "knee-jerk" reasons people say "no" when first presented with a proposition ever to accept that as their final answer. Think about something as simple as entering a store and instantly being confronted by a sales clerk: "Can I help you find something?" This is a spectacularly unproductive although frightfully common retail sales tactic. The overwhelming majority of customers say "No, just looking," even if they *aren't* just browsing, *are* after something specific, and *could* use help. Why? Too soon. Aversion to being sold. Deal with self to compare at several stores before buying. Lots of reasons. A clerk identifying herself and NOT directly seeking engagement – "Hi, I'm Melanie. If I can be of any assistance, you'll find me over by the blue counter" and then, seven to ten minutes later, approaching – "Hi, just checking in. May I help you find something?" has a four hundred percent better chance of getting a "yes." And the third time's the charm: roughly sixty percent of shoppers accept help after a greeting plus two requests. All that's research validated, by the way.

Often, you get different answers from different people at the same company or agency. Robert Ringer taught me: if you're on the phone getting a "no" from some faceless cubicle dweller at a big company or bureaucracy, dis-engage, call back, get a different cubicle dweller, and start over. It's more productive than battling to the death with the first one. People in zero incentive jobs, paid the same no matter what, tend to say "no" more than "yes" and say it quickly, principally because saying "no" is easier and safer than saying "yes," doesn't create work for them, and may even satisfy a resentment they harbor for their employer or for the customers. The bureaucratic, automatic, mindless "no" is their revenge.

My own number-one gripe with my own key employees over all the years has been how easily they accept a "no" – or any other undesirable answer – from a vendor or vendor's employees. For what it's worth here is my favorite lecture on this subject:

> When I task you with getting repair service out to the office today and you tell me that they said they can't come until next Tuesday, you have failed, and in all likelihood you failed easily, taking the very first "can't"

as the answer, from whoever first talked with you. Stopping when the first pebble bumps up against your shoe is no way to climb a mountain. Remember that "can't" doesn't mean "can't." They have trucks, tools, and repair people. They "can" get one over here two minutes ago. If the president of their company had his witzabib-bitis go perflunk, they wouldn't tell him he had to wait until next Tuesday, would they? Of course not. Well, I'll bet his is still humming along, so they can send over the guy they'd rush over to his place if his did quit. Can't means won't, and you are being paid to change won't to can and will, no to yes. In case you didn't know it before, you do now – that's your job description: changing "no" to "yes" so we get what we need and want when we need and want it. Don't take the first "no." If you can't get a "yes" from the first person, move on up the ladder. Don't accept failure.

And, here's my second lecture on the same subject:

You're fired.

Harsh? I suppose so. But ultimately you have to decide whether to be a loser or a winner and whether to surround yourself with and depend on losers or winners. Losers have one thing in common: losing. The more losing they accept or get accepted, the more easily they surrender the next time. It starts with accepting the first no. It morphs to starting out suggesting it – "I imagine you'll say no to this, but…" It ends with not even trying.

By the way, we have a little dog, affectionately, and world-famously known as "the million dollar dog." She rarely accepts the first "no" about anything: treat, belly rub, walk, foray out onto backyard deck to bark. She understands "no." She just doesn't *buy it*. Which gets to an important truth: in every interchange between two people, selling is going on, and a sale gets made. One sells, the other buys. If you buy a no, you failed and the other person succeeded at making a sale. You bought what you didn't want; she sold what she wanted you to buy. Seriously, is this how you want to go through life? If not, you'll learn to sell your way through life.

No is a voluntarily accepted verdict.

There are basically only two things standing between you and whatever you want: people saying "no" and you accepting their "no"s.

NO IS A VOLUNTARILY ACCEPTED VERDICT.

10 DON'T MAKE – OR ACCEPT – EXCUSES

(Dan)

I have a couple beliefs about accomplishment of all kinds, but since this is largely a business and money book, I'll narrow to that. The first is admittedly observational and very un-scientific, but if you have unwed daughters, pass it on. The better a dancer a guy is, the less money he'll ever make. Unless he's a dance studio owner.

The other one is more validated, based on more experience, with more people, over more years, and I present it with unequivocal certainty. The better a person is at making excuses, the less able he is to make money. These two skills and habits are mutually exclusive. If you permit yourself excuse making, you rob yourself of power. You really need to police this tendency in yourself.

Not making excuses for yourself also grants you moral authority for intolerance for others' excuses. If you permit yourself to be surrounded by excuse-makers, you'll drown in their sewage. Excuse-making staff, associates, vendors add too much dead weight for anybody to carry very far. Get those who will stop; get rid of those who won't. When an excuse is uttered, write it down. Explain to the excuse-maker that the excuses on the paper are not acceptable. They are only proof that the excuse-maker needs to be replaced by a results-producer.

Vendors must be educated that their machinery malfunctions, their absent employees, their floods and fires, their late nights, their problems are theirs. Not yours. Theirs. If you wanted to own them, solve them, or even hear about them, you would own their businesses too. You do not. You pay for performance as promised.

YOU PAY FOR PERFORMANCE AS PROMISED.

Employees must be educated in the same way. Take note of Chapter 6, about accepting "no"s. You pay for performance. Why there is failure is really quite irrelevant. Failure earns no reward. Why a person is late doesn't matter to you. Their house, car, dog, spouse--all their problems. Not yours. Theirs. Your only concern is their reliability, their honoring of their agreements with you, their performance.

If an employee or a vendor came into your office several times a week or more often, maybe in response to every task, and smeared a pile of fresh manure onto your face or desktop or carpet, how long would you let that go on? That's what an excuse is. Manure. That's what you do to yourself when you make excuses. It's what you let others do when they deliver excuses.

For more, read my book, *NO B.S. RUTHLESS MANAGEMENT OF PEOPLE AND PROFITS.*

People who make or accept excuses are rich in only one thing: excuses.

In his original work *Laws of Success*, preceding the more famous condensation, *Think and Grow Rich*, Napoleon Hill wrote at length about the effect of "habit-force" even on strong-willed people. We are routine makers by our very nature. After a short time, you adopt an order for your morning bathroom and dressing ritual, and then follow it by habit morning after morning after morning. All kinds of behavior evolve into habit and are then governed by habit. We are also habitual with regard to thinking. Habits of reactive thought to various stimuli evolve and then govern. We think we are thinking when actually we are merely re-playing pre-recorded thought by sheer habit, as a stimulus calls for. That's why excuse making is so dangerous. It doesn't take doing it much before the subconscious mind decides it's a desired response to all sorts of stimuli. That response of excuse-making quickly becomes habit. If you already have this habit, it won't be easy to break and replace with a more productive one. It will take conscious awareness and real discipline. As Hill said, the chains of habit-force are invisible yet stronger and harder to break than the giant metal chains mooring a freighter to a dock.

There's another thing. A lot of people *prefer* a good excuse to opportunity and achievement. If someone is a habitual non-achiever or under-achiever, demonstrating little or no forward progress year to year, he must explain that to himself and others. Standing up and saying "I have no sincere ambition and am unwilling to manage myself for achievement" is probably *not* going to be the chosen explanation. Someone who is defeated in life doesn't want to shoulder the blame – he or she wants to affix blame elsewhere. This is considered politically incorrect, insensitive and unkind to say, but saying anything else only serves to further imprison. The jailer is the excuse making. Liberty can only be had by accepting responsibility. The starting point of all achievement is acceptance of responsibility for the intended achievement and for self.

This entire chapter has been rough. Harsh. *True.*

A LOT OF PEOPLE PREFER A GOOD EXCUSE TO OPPORTUNITY AND ACHIEVEMENT.

Now I want to let you in on a little secret about my business and Ben's. We guide people to getting rich and all that goes with it: success, independence, freedom. Truth be told, fewer than five percent of lawyers achieve these high goals. About fifteen percent more achieve significant benefits by their association with us. Eighty percent, not so much. The reasons why somebody is in the five percent, the fifteen percent, or the eighty percent have very little to do with us, though, and much to do with them. And there are reliable predictors. The person who has a lot of excuses why our stuff can't work for them in their practices, why their staff won't let them use our stuff, why they're too busy to even study our stuff, etc., etc. has a lot of excuses why nothing else works for them either and a lot of excuses why they don't get ahead – this person is an able excuse-maker rich in excuses and *therefore* guaranteed to stay poor in everything else no matter who or what he comes in contact with along the way. Opportunity can't save him. Coaching won't help him. The person who is determined to dig in, study, find, apply, use, and profit from all he can does very well with us. But, you see, that's more about that person than about us. Isn't that an interesting secret?

11 DON'T SCREW WITH ME

(Ben)

I have a competitor in my "neighborhood" who I know talks bad about me behind my back, posts stupid stuff on list serves about me, and is generally envious of the work that I do and of the fact that I've got a MasterMind member who competes with him. Every once in a while, he contacts me, playing nice, and wants my input on some marketing tool. He's never curious, mind you, about the one hundred questions I would be asking someone about this – questions like: Where did you get the idea? Who else uses it? What did you have to do to set it up? What's the follow up? Who do you use to produce your books and videos and how the hell do you get it all done?

He just wants to know, "Should I invest in this product/service?" I was sorely tempted to tell him "yes" a week ago and watch him go piss away all of his money just copying what he thinks he sees me doing (a fool's game).

But... I'm a nice guy and I just can't resist helping him play in the big leagues, so here was my response:

Dear [ ]:

Yes, I still use [particular service]. Please understand that this is only one small part of a very complex marketing machine that I have built over the last 12 years. I have found that there is no one thing that I do that drives 7,000 unique visitor to just one of my web properties a month and there is no ONE thing I do to convert them to clients. I have written 15 books that I use; I DO employ 3 people whose sole jobs are to produce content, including video for my sites; and I do get up every morning at 4:30 to make sure that I do at least one NEW thing every day to drive people down my funnel. Most recently, I have opened 7 branch offices, including one right in your neighborhood. That office is currently my most productive branch office and I'm out there one day each week just to meet new clients, so I do know that there are a lot of people in your neck of the woods who are looking for personal injury lawyers. So, yes, by all means, invest in [particular service].

Hugs, Ben

P.S. I won't be going to the AAJ meeting in Phoenix because I was just in Phoenix a few months ago meeting with my attorney marketing MasterMind members. I came back from that meeting with 23 new things to test and implement. I hope you find your trip there just as fruitful. Phoenix is beautiful.

DON'T PUNT

(Dan)

Every NFL coach knows the rule-book's instructions about NOT going for it on fourth down, especially if it's fourth and long, especially if backed up toward one's own goal posts. However, the highest paid, most celebrated, winningest coaches, with very rare exception, go for it on fourth more than the mediocre majority, the journeyman coaches who move from bad team to bad team, who never win the big games. If you punt on every fourth down, you may do "okay." But only "okay."

In life, in business, always punting is even more damaging, even less rewarding. Fortune favors the bold, the decisive, the responsible; the person who takes it on himself and risks financial and personal damage on decisions often viewed as unwise or unpopular by others, including experts. You can hide in the mediocre-middle by punting every difficult decision away. You can't score doing that.

Here is a very valid explanation, from the richest man in the U.K. that you've never heard of, of why some of us get rich but so many others – with more education, knowledge, ability or talent – do not. "Many employees think they are smarter than their bosses, and, although I'm usually loathe to admit it, truth is, they are. But smarts so very, very, very rarely equal success or power. The boss isn't the boss because he's so much smarter than everybody else. These same employees feel they are under-paid and are entitled to much more because their boss is so much dumber than they are. Here, they are wrong. There is a reason he has the two mansions, five cars, and millions in the bank and they don't." That reason – embrace of responsibility. Willingness to risk, make mistakes, fix things.

Should you prefer to play it safe – and coach by the book, punt-ing every fourth down – then you need to accept the inevita-ble and decreed-by-universal- risk/reward- law result and quit complaining about it. You decide to be a drone. And that's per-fectly okay. Please be the best drone you can and do the best you can as a drone. But don't expect otherwise. And stop asking the government to steal my money gotten through risk and give it to you without it being earned by risk. That's immoral. May everyone who refuses to risk but demands the rewards of those who do and begs for handouts get a kick in the ass from the devil in the afterlife.

You have talent. God shorted no one. If you live in America, you were gifted the best possible birthright: massive opportunity. Should you choose to squander both in favor of avoiding bruises, that's your right. Just get real about your choices.

YOU HAVE TALENT.

13 DON'T WORRY TOO MUCH ABOUT WHAT "OTHERS" THINK ABOUT YOU

(Dan)

Hypersensitivity equals inhibition, which retards ambition, initiative, creativity, and action.

Hypersensitivity about what others think about you – particularly others who do not directly affect your income or forward progress to your goals – is a form of mental illness. It is as much a sickness as would be endlessly worrying about the clothes you choose to wear around the house offending, disappointing, or being gossiped about by your house plants and goldfish. If they have opinions, so what?

Productive, profitable sensitivity has a logic to it, although even it can be carried too far. Consider a group of five hundred businesspeople in Louisville, Kentucky, at a hotel, milling about in the lobby through which I am going to walk, accompanied by and talking with two associates. Do I care what these people may think about what I'm wearing or what they might overhear me saying? If they are soon to be in an audience I'll be speaking to, to sell something to, yes I care. If not, I do not. And, actually, I care only about those in the five hundred who will buy from me. When I do speak, I will offend some, and likely a few will leave early; I call these "deliberate sacrifices" – in order to achieve faster, clearer rapport with my most likely buyers. The fact that a non-buyer goes home and tells his wife about that jerk who was speaking in Louisville matters not one whit to me. This is what is called pragmatic immunity to criticism. The opposite is a very thin skin.

Although a bit of this truth has eroded since his move to the relative oblivion of satellite radio, Howard Stern was and may still be among the very top, highest income, wealthiest radio personalities in America. Right next to him, the highest paid and richest radio personality: Rush Limbaugh. They are also among the most criticized, most frequently criticized, and most vehemently and viciously criticized. I doubt either loses sleep over the critics' opinions. Jerry Lewis famously proclaimed that women comedians aren't funny and can't be funny. It is widely believed that the remark was aimed at Joan Rivers. His opinion did not affect her career, nor impede countless other female comedians since. Chelsea Handler, for example, has been piling up mountains of money from TV, tours and *New York Times* bestselling books, seemingly undeterred by Jerry's expert opinion. The public has ignored his opinion as well. As it is with a lot of critical opinion: the buying public ignores it. Routine for a movie to garner unanimously horrible reviews but be number-one at the box office and rake in many tens of millions of dollars. Some of the most popular and highest earning actors and other entertainers get the least awards and poorest critical acclaim. There's a truth that carries over to business and suggests a counter-intuitive strategy.

I am aware that I annoy a whole lot of people. Some because I outright target them by name or type or category – as in my books. Others because of philosophical positions. Others because I am successful and they are less so. They feel my success is unjust since they have superior academic credentials, skill, or talent. Others simply because of style issues--the way I express myself. On the Internet, in what Google's CEO correctly termed a "cesspool," there are, I'm told, entire web sites and forums devoted to critics of mine leading on-going discussions about what a schmuck, arrogant s.o.b., charlatan, etc. I am. Everybody's free to have opinions. I'm free to ignore them.

> **EVERYBODY'S FREE TO HAVE OPINIONS. I'M FREE TO IGNORE THEM.**

Criticism comes with anything much more aggressive than curling up in a ball in your mother's basement and never showing yourself in the light of day. Assuming you venture out at all, you *are* going to be criticized, disliked, gossiped about, lied about, and otherwise crapped on – the only questions are about quantity, frequency, ferociousness, and what you decide to think about it all. Of prime importance, the quantity, frequency, and ferociousness goes up in corollary to expressed ambition, initiative, and achievement.

The actor appearing only in community theater productions in his home town in the middle of Indiana is extremely unlikely to be ripped in a scathing review by the theater critic of the *New York Times* nor ambushed by the TMZ paparazzi when exiting his local pub a bit sloshed, wearing women's underthings on his head. Only if he rises to starring roles on Broadway will he be the object of such attention. Further, the critic in his hometown paper is likely to be gentle even if his performance sucks – after all, the newspaper gets needed ad dollars from the theater, and everybody bumps into each other at Mabel's Diner. The *New York Times* critic may viciously eviscerate the Broadway actor even if his performance does not suck – the standards are higher, the critic is immune from advertiser pressure, and may very well hate talented actors. Of course, the actor who stays in his hometown or, at most daring, steps up to traveling dinner theater troupes working small towns throughout the Midwest, will never grow rich from acting.

The question most often asked, after I go through all this, is: okay, I get all that – but is it NECESSARY to be criticized and gossiped about and disliked, and NECESSARY to offend and annoy people in order to be exceptionally successful?

In one of my advanced trainings called "The 7-Figures Academy," for people earning or seeking to earn seven-figure incomes, i.e. one or more million dollars per year, I answer it: you don't have to *be* an a-hole, but you do have to be willing to be thought of and spoken of as an a-hole by some, maybe by many; you may even need to encourage it, and you must be unaffected by it.

Ronald Reagan was one of the most popular, most liked, and now most fondly remembered U.S. presidents. Even determined political foes from the opposition party, notably then-Speaker of the House Tip O'Neil found him too genial and pleasant to dislike, and the two men frequently sat down privately for day-end cocktails. While very much opposed to his politics, Walter Mondale found himself unable to attack Reagan, and Reagan easily handled him in presidential debates. However, memory fades of how harsh and foul and vitriolic media figures and entire media outlets were in their attacks on Ronald Reagan and on his wife, Nancy. And there were and are plenty of people, including political figures, pundits, comedians who absolutely despise Reagan, call him the worst of all presidents, and still grab every opportunity to paint him as a fool and buffoon or a tool of the rich or a destroyer of justice. For many years, the Reagans could not open a newspaper without reading criticism. It comes with the territory. By comparison to being the president of the United States, being Bill Maher or Jon Stewart or Chris Matthews is the equivalent of being a tiny speck of dog poop stuck on the foot of a centipede. Yet they manage to make a lot of noise. Anyone deterred or depressed by that noise simply can't function as president. So it is with anyone in any important, responsible role, at any level: if deterred or depressed by the noise, you cannot function.

Purely from a business point of view, the simple truth is this: rarely do critics or criticism define a business or determine its success or failure. Criticism can ebb and flow like tides, and be more bothersome or even dangerous at some times or another, but its greatest danger is in being given greater power than it inherently possesses. Critics and criticism are almost never powerful enough to determine outcomes for a business. *Only customers are that powerful.* So the astute business owner has very high immunity to criticism from everybody but customers, and pays obsessive attention to the needs, desires, experiences, thoughts, and feelings of his customers.

DAN'S RESPONSES TO FOOLISH CRITICISM

Courtesy of Dr. Charlie Jarvis:

Dear Sir/Madam,

I am writing to let you know some idiot has stolen some of your letterhead and is using it to send out moronic letters purportedly from you. I wish you luck in tracking this lunatic down.

For Criticism Disguised as Offer to Help

Dear Sir/Madam,

I appreciate your generous offer of copious advice about my speaking/writing/web sites/whatever, which I have spent 30 years mastering and had the good fortune of making tens of millions of dollars from and becoming celebrated worldwide as expert in.

I'll be happy to meet with you. Please bring the last 3 years of your tax returns and other proof of your income from speaking/writing/web sites/whatever.

I'll show you mine if you'll show me yours. If you are making more from this than I am, well, then I'm all ears. I'll even pay you for your advice.

DON'T JUST WAIT FOR CLIENTS TO COME TO YOU

(Ben)

I saw an interesting article in the *Wall Street Journal*. A 68-year-old grandmother was described as one of the most prolific salespeople on earth. Her name is Holly Chen and she is into Amway. Turns out that one in ten Amway reps are in her "herd." I don't know much about how Amway works, but the $8,000,000 she makes a year should make you curious about how she thinks.

No need to wonder how she thinks. She is quoted in the article as saying, "I always think Amway is a system that's designed by God, only for me…So when you are in the Amway business, of course you change your mindset, you change your attitude, and your *outcome will definitely change with it.*"

I do harp on this mindset and attitude thing a lot, because most of us have just a couple of points of leverage in our businesses. If you've been practicing law for a few years now, it is unlikely that you can become a four times better lawyer by study or even by fifteen more years of experience. Maybe you can, but it is unlikely. (Truth be told, being a better lawyer than the next lawyer in town isn't a marketing advantage, anyway. The public can't tell one from the other until YOU teach them. That's a different lesson, however.)

You can, however, vastly change your own "outcome" by changing two things: your marketing skill level and your attitude. In our statewide legal newspaper, *Lawyers Weekly Virginia*, there are usually two pages of verdict and settlement reports. My attitude is: "I should have gotten all of those cases…how did THEIR marketing snag them?" Hence, my devotion of considerable time and resources not only to improving the essential Ben Glass Law "Internet footprint" (including hiring more freelance web developers and writers through Elance for some of our "smaller" web properties), but also creating a way to market effectively for cases statewide by opening 16 satellite offices in the last 16 months. Knowing what to do, marketing-wise, and combining it with a "dammit, we should be able to get all of those cases" attitude could add millions to your bank account. It can become almost turn-key. (Several of my MasterMind members are now opening satellite offices, as well, and are reporting very high client satisfaction response with this strategy.)

You've got to at least have THIS attitude about marketing: *There are folks out there who need me...really need me...I am the perfect lawyer for them (and they are the perfect client for me). It is my DUTY to make sure they don't fall into the hands of some hack lawyer.* If you don't believe that YOU are the PERFECT lawyer for some folks (not all), then why not get out now? I hear there's an Amway spot open in your town.

> ## "THERE ARE FOLKS OUT THERE WHO NEED ME"

DON'T OVER-INFLATE THE IMPORTANCE OF ANY ONE THING

(Dan)

I confess to watching the movie *Hudson Hawk* at least thirty times. It is so incredibly, unbelievably, embarrassingly awful it is much funnier than it was intended to be. If you've missed this classic, it appears on cable from time to time. Bruce Willis and Danny Aiello star as cat burglars who sing while burgling – with full orchestra music behind them – in order to time their heists, Andie McDowell as a nun/art curator/Willis's love interest, James Coburn as a CIA bad guy, and two actors whose names I forget as silly villains. There's also a butler with carving knives that snap out of his cuffs. Oh, and did I mention that Bruce Willis *sings*.

Everybody who accomplishes much of anything has at least one *Hudson Hawk* in his or her life.

This movie ended none of these actors' careers.

If I were ever to run for public office, the first four hours of my announcement speech would be used up revealing all the dirty linen in the closet. Personally, I've had an alcohol problem, had two cars repossessed, gone bankrupt, been thrown out of a major trade association for so-called ethics violations, and am twice divorced. If we add the disclosures about relatives' stints in jail, their naked, drunken gun-fighting in the street, etc., and business associates who (a) stuck up a bank and (b) disappeared in the dead of night (we think across the border to Mexico, never to be seen again) at different times, we've got a thick catalog of uglies. It wouldn't be enough to get you impeached, but it might get in your way campaigning, even though the standards *are* turning into a limbo game on the beach: how low can you go?

Anyway, a number of those incidents of mine – and others not listed here - seemed at first to be of life-and-death importance, career ending significance, ruinous calamities from which no recovery could be possible and shame would be eternal.

Turns out none of them matter now or mattered much even within days, weeks, or months, and if I'd stop mentioning them, they'd have long ago gone away altogether.

NONE OF THEM MATTER NOW

When teenagers have that first big break-up with the first serious girlfriend or boyfriend, they all consider driving their Chevies to the levy to end it all. And, incidentally, teen suicide is a near epidemic in this country. Much of it has to do with youthful inexperience and lack of any perspective whatsoever, so that any single adverse event is so magnified in importance it is unbearable. It's important to leave that drama behind when you depart high school.

Harvey MacKay put together a great book titled *WE GOT FIRED!* that chronicles the firings of now famous people, the rich, the very rich, the famous, the celebrated, the respected. Another book on financial fiascos profiles many of the most successful entrepreneurs' bankruptcies and near bankruptcies. Imagine that – *entire books* full of rich and famous people who got fired or went broke or both, recovered, and went on to bigger and better things.

Richard Branson is, at the moment, one of the world's most famous entrepreneurs and entrepreneurial heroes. His rags to riches story legend, his Virgin brand extended over dozens of high-flying businesses, his persona larger than life. Neither he nor others talk much about the more than fifty businesses he has started, attached the Virgin brand to, failed with, and abandoned. And really, who cares? I've seen Branson interviewed on TV on various financial shows at least a hundred times and can recall none where this aspect of his biography has ever been raised. Nobody mentions his one season-and-cancelled attempt at copycatting Trump's hugely successful *The Apprentice* TV franchise either.

Vanessa Williams had her beauty queen crown forcibly removed after nude, lesbian photos appeared in *Penthouse* magazine, at a time such a thing was still scandalous. Today, she has a very successful singing and acting career and has made a fortune hosting my client, Guthy-Renker's, Pro-Activ infomercials. Did her scandal matter? If so, temporarily, and more in her mind than anywhere else. For better or worse, the former governor of New York, who resigned in disgrace after caught consorting with the very kind of escort service-provided prostitutes he had previously made himself famous prosecuting landed on CNN as prime-time political news commentator. Not the Comedy Channel. CNN.

My friend Sydney Barrows was plastered all over the New York City media when arrested for running the city's then most successful, highest priced, very upscale escort service. Because of her blue-blood genealogy, she was dubbed by the media as "the Mayflower Madam." Her financial position ruined, her name trashed, after narrowly escaping doing prison time, she started her life over. That was many years ago. She has since established herself as a business author, speaker, and coach, in several subject areas, including "creating extraordinary customer experiences." You may write your own joke. I chose instead to write a book with her, *Uncensored Sales Strategies*, which I un-humbly recommend. Her admittedly unusual "credential" is too valuable to let go of, so despite all the time elapsed, it remains part of her bio and story to this day, and she has had to get comfortable with life experience that, pardon my pun, arouses curiosity, and for extremely astute businesspeople, arouses purposed, productive curiosity. Her back-story causes snickers, snide remarks, and skepticism, but it also is rich with rare lessons in the marketing of intangibles (because the business was *not* as simple as selling sex), the establishment of trust with affluent clientele, what she now calls Sales Choreography®, and price strategy. Another area of discussion she engages clients in, for which her fall and re-making prepared her, is the removal of mental blocks built from past or present in order to liberate achievement. If you like, you can find her at SydneyBarrows.com.

When your disaster is the front page of the *New York Post* and the *New York Daily News* days or weeks running, the fodder for late-night comedians, the subject of news pundits' discussions, perhaps preserved forever in living color on YouTube, you're in a special fraternity. These are very public rises, crashes, and recoveries. We watch them played out in the media as larger than life reality TV shows. But in not-so-famous peoples' personal and business lives, similar falls into very muddy waters occur frequently, often publicly viewed in their local communities, within their industries, or by some audience. Most successful people get beat up, bruised, and bloodied more than once along the way.

I'm a big egg on face guy. I can show you past and recent embarrassing and messy business flops requiring apologies all around, clean-ups on aisles 3 through 30. Hasn't mattered. But the willingness to endure them has mattered a great deal. It has permitted me to risk, and in some cases, the risk has paid off very handsomely. It's very, very, very hard to get rich and richer, or even to stay rich, entirely safe. It's important that I understand that our two homes, my "toy" classic cars, my private flying, my racehorses, and the demand for me as author, speaker, consultant, business partner is not a product only of my good judgment and successful achievements, but just as much product of all my bad judgment and markedly unsuccessful and at times humiliating and painful experiences. I keep reminding myself of that with each new mark on that second post.

My passion – driving professionally some two hundred times a year in harness races – is not without egg on face. Unconfirmed but believed true, that I hold the all-time record, having had my license yanked not once but twice by racing officials before securing it and now holding it for more than ten years on the third go-round. And the two losses weren't quiet. They were public spectacles, on the racetrack, in front of hundreds of fans and the entire colony of horsemen each time. Without generous lobbying on my behalf by a couple leading drivers at the time and my trainer-partner using up most of his political capital, and groveling by me, I'd have never gotten licensed. But that was a decade ago. Few remember. And it does not matter at all to me or anybody else. It is as if it never occurred. Racing is continuously humbling, by the way, because you lose more than you win, and most races leave you playing the shoulda/coulda game; some weeks leave you wondering why the hell you're doing this and whether or not you should be; but a couple wins in a row erase all that.

The same is true in everything. A couple wins in a row erase all that has come before – no matter how ruinous it seemed at its moment. Winning IS everything. Losing is almost never permanent unless you surrender.

In today's world, six months is an eternity. If you pay attention, you'll see person after person, institution after institution get caught in some mess of seemingly epic proportions, but six months later it's distant memory and inconsequential. During the months I was working on this book, for example, a major fast food chain became the focus of news exposé, sparking government investigation, civil litigation, and Jay Leno jokes nightly, for having only thirty percent beef in what it advertised as the beef in its beefy tacos and burritos. This was THE news for a couple weeks. You'd think it would wound this company for years, maybe destroy it. I did a little, informal test as I was finishing this chapter: I named the chain to fifteen different people including, mostly, people who probably patronize it from time to time and asked them to tell me of anything that had been in the news about the restaurant chain in past months. Zero for fifteen. Frankly, I don't think the public's shortening memory and remarkably blasé attitudes about politicians', corporations', and others' disreputable behavior, malfeasance, lousy judgment and scandals are a good thing. But if *you* get caught with your pants down, hand in cookie jar, and embarrassing photos of it all tweeted about, you can take solace in this reality. Take just a six-month vacation and it'll be safe to start your comeback.

Let's be optimists and assume you are *not* going to be the darling of TMZ and YouTube and the nightly news for some spectacular peccadillo. Let's bring this down to the day-to-day events, the ups and downs, the seeming crisis of the week. **One of my most basic business principles is: *nothing* is ever as bad – or good – as it first appears.** Like all absolutist statements, if you're really picky and determined, you can cite examples that defy that principle. But for the most part, it's true. Further, whatever is occurring right in front of you and has your attention of the moment is seen through a magnifying glass. That's what attention and concentration creates: magnification. The danger of magnification is that an ordinary housefly unknowingly viewed through a powerful magnifying pane of glass can give you a heart attack. Magnification of trouble can blind you to solutions and opportunities, resulting in paralysis. Dr. Edward Kramer's great quote applies: a penny held to the eye blocks the entire sun.

Comedy teaches us this lesson. With only a handful of historical examples, even the most dire tragedies have become fodder for jokes and comedy we find funny, given enough time-distance from the tragedy. Almost every rich person I know has stories to tell of his most desperate times that he now finds funny, but were utterly devoid of humor when he was broke and struggling with them. Time-distance relieves the pressure of intense magnification and permits, in its place, perspective. The first dictionary definition of perspective is: the art of drawing solid objects on a two-dimensional surface so as to give the right impression of their height, width, depth, and position in relation to each other when viewed from a particular point. Similarly, we might define perspective as thinking, rather than drawing, about life events rather than physical objects, that conveys a fair and accurate impression of their relative importance to other life events. In both cases – drawing or thinking – it's a skill.

Extremely resilient people, quickly resilient people have the skill of perspective without requiring the lapse of time and time-distance from the situation. That is far easier observed and stated than practiced. Nonetheless, it's a success secret of those who take on much and handle it with apparent aplomb.

What happens to you happens to you, and may or may not have been avoidable or preventable, all or mostly or nominally your fault, may be unfair and unjust and undeserved, and may inflict some damage. These things are then almost certainly true about it: one, as magnification is mitigated with perspective, its importance and its power over you will wane – so whatever you can do to hurry the perspective, the better. Two, it is most assuredly not your unique, one of a kind, never before occurring crisis or disaster or scandal or illness or whatever. Others have come around the very same corner too fast, spun out and hit the same damn tree. Seek out those who recovered. Find them directly or via interviews, articles, books, or films. Hear their thoughts and study their experiences, and use them to hurry your perspective and encourage your resilience. Three, whatever has happened, what you now think about it and do about it will prove infinitely more important than what others may think about it and about you, and more important than the thing itself.

I woke up and my girl asked if I slept well. "No," I said, "I made a couple of mistakes."

- Steven Wright

DON'T SCREW WITH ME, PART 2
(OUR HYDRA GREW 7 HEADS EVERY TIME)

(Ben)

A couple years ago, our Google Places website for the Fairfax office of Ben Glass Law had about four reviews. Each was more than a year old. We started a program in house to increase the number and quality of reviews. My staff and I developed a system for going after these reviews from everyone we talked to or emailed or "live chatted" with.

It worked. We started to get more and more reviews and "5 stars" from folks we had been able to help in some way. Then something interesting happened: we attracted the attention of a nut job. One day, my son, Brian, mentioned, "You are getting flamed on Google." Whoa… a bunch of not only negative reviews, but totally false reviews. "We hired Ben Glass to do our divorce. He's all over billboards in Northern Virginia, but he treated us like dirt." (For anyone new to GLM, we don't do divorce cases and there are exactly "0" billboards gracing the highways and byways of Northern Virginia.) The "reviews" were always posted by a first-name-only person and when you checked, this was the only review this person had ever posted. Because the newest reviews appear at the top of the table, this was a big "ouch." It was also, frankly, depressing. (Read Loral Langemeier's *Yes, Energy*. In it, she describes exactly the same thing happening to her business at one time. Her response – gee, this must be a sign of success – was encouraging.)

We contacted brother "Google" and they were of no help, sending me an autoresponder email that landed in my inbox exactly three seconds after I hit "send" on their detailed "tell us about false reviews and we'll take care of it report," telling me basically that after "investigation of my complaint," I could go screw myself.

At the same time that we were banging our heads against the Google brick wall (note to self: cancel what little pay-per-click ads and sponsored videos we were experimenting with), we went to our herd. We reached out to our BGL "maven" list and to the GLM MasterMinds and said, "Some nut job is posting false reviews at Google; if you are so inclined, could you chime in?"

Bang! We now have the most reviews of any law firm in Northern Virginia and we were able not only to push the false ones down the page, but shame the idiot (we think this was a local competitor who is extremely jealous that everywhere he looks he sees me and my buddies) into going away (knock on wood).

You can't do this without cultivating a herd of people who know you, trust you, and will evangelize for you. (Of course, you have to have a way of segregating the list and getting your message out quickly – thank you, InfusionSoft and BaseCamp.) This is not built on "advertising," but on relationships built over time, in person, and in writing. It is built on authenticity.

IT IS BUILT ON AUTHENTICITY.

DON'T OVER-INFLATE THE IMPORTANCE OF ANY ONE PERSON

(Dan)

Martin and Lewis were THE hottest, most famous, highest paid comedy team of their moments in time. Their bitter break-up was viewed by just about everybody who mattered in the entertainment industry, their close friends and advisors, and the public, as the end for both of them. Some thought Jerry might survive without Dean; no one thought Dean could survive without Jerry.

Wrong. Both went on to fabulous, multi-dimensional careers, both became fabulously wealthy.

Regis Philbin, who has logged more hours in front of TV cameras than any other entertainer according to the *Guinness Book of World Records*, has run through a long line of interchangeable female co-hosts. Kathie Lee who?

Dick Wolf, television producer and owner of the immensely valuable *Law & Order* shows franchise has made the actors interchangeable cogs in his machine. And whatever happened to Michael Moriarty?

The 007 franchise has never *quite* been what it was with Sean Connery. But it has still made an absolute ton of money for its owners, using and discarding three successors to its current fourth (if you don't count Woody Allen as Bond in his version of *Casino Royale*).

And it will probably out-live its original star.

Admittedly neither the Captain nor Tenille has had a solo career. But Cher's done just fine absent Sonny.

Starbucks suffered from the absence of founder Howard Schultz. In 2006-2007 over half of its stock value disappeared. Howard returned and is succeeding at reinvigorating the brand. But McDonald's did not miss a beat post-Kroc. Actually more companies built from the ground up by entrepreneurs prosper more after the founder gives up control than during his or her control. Companies liberated of their founders' biases often enjoy explosive growth, broad diversification and lucrative expansion. Even Walt Disney proved non-essential to the company he created and for which he was heart, soul, pater familias, and public face.

Quarterbacks certainly matter in the NFL. But Joe Gibbs won a Super Bowl with an off-the-bench, limping, previously uncelebrated Doug Williams throwing the ball. And both Tom Landry at Dallas and Bill Walsh at the 49'ers built systems teams, more akin to Dick Wolf's *Law & Order* than to star-powered teams like the Colts with Peyton Manning. It was a plus having Montana, but it wasn't necessary. In sports, it's common to think of someone as irreplaceable – but that person rarely is. In Green Bay, the entire city thought, who could ever replace Brett Favre? Go see how many fans are wearing jerseys with Aaron Rodgers's number on it. There was fear that the popularity of golf would die with the aging of Arnold Palmer and Jack Nicklaus. But along came Tiger. He has self-destructed. If he cannot get back?

NO ONE IS IRREPLACEABLE

Golf will survive. No one is irreplaceable to a sport or a team or a company. If Walt Disney wasn't irreplaceable, no one is irreplaceable.

In my life, I've lost partners, key employees (including one who my competitor thought would bring all her accounts with her and was sadly disappointed), friends, and wives. Some of these losses have far greater *meaning* than others. But none has been fatal. No organization's loss of a person need be cataclysmic. No one person's loss of another is fatal unless the disaffected departing fires a gun at you in exit and is a good shot.

The more you do, the more you accomplish, the more you are out there, the more people will come and go through your doors. At times, you will feel inseparably bonded with them. At times, you will feel desperately in need of them. At times you will feel unable to go on without them. These feelings can be very acute. But they are feelings about reality, not reality about reality. No loss of any person can actually destroy you or destroy an organization. In business relationships (at least), my saying from the racetrack is: they ALL go lame. It is a rare, rare, rare, rare, race horse that goes its entire career to mandatory retirement at age fourteen without a career ending physical lameness, a value ending loss of competitive will to win, a transition from consistent to erratic performance. They all go lame. It is question of when, not if. Thus you must always be prepared to load them into the trailer, pat 'em on the ass one last time, send 'em down the road to a different place and activity, and forget 'em— to focus instead on the ones you've got.

It's a bad idea to bet your Barbie money on ANY relationship going the whole distance.

A far better and more sensible wager is on the relationship not surviving. The way you make that insurance bet, by the way, is with a pre-nup, in personal or business life, with every relationship. Negotiate the exit before anyone can imagine wanting it. I tell you this, as most who will tell you this do, from bitter personal experience of failing to do so. Once.

I am a pragmatist about this. I also have made myself a very self-confident and self-reliant individual, and cannot ever recall *long* feeling incapacitated by loss of any one person. By far, the worst ever was divorce from Carla. But I *functioned*. And I began recovery sooner, not later.

The price is emotional distance. Most high achieving entrepreneurs have it. Most people who don't are, at some point, emotionally and practically crippled by some loss of friend, ally, associate, benefactor, or even enemy. (When President Reagan finished the busting up of the Soviet Union, a high-ranking executive at the largest of the military contractors reportedly said, "Now look at what that idiot has done. Without the Russian threat, we'll be out of business and selling pencils on street corners in a year." By the way, a lot of people thought Reagan an idiot, for different reasons. All were wrong.)

Like a swooning teen, Angelina Jolie tattooed Billy Bob's name on her skin with his blood, or some such thing. They bit each other and drank each other's blood. She pronounced him her only possible soul mate in this or any other lifetime. Today, the whole episode is a distant memory. The tattoo, I believe, expensively and painfully removed. It actually *was* only skin deep.

There are many ways to think about this. One is with fear. Another, melancholy and sadness. The other, a somewhat metaphysical view, is as a series of adventures, opportunities for new and different experiences, even for "trading up." You can appreciate the time you had with whoever, but you dare not feel as if that person was essential to your well-being. You lived and laughed and made money before that person, you can do so after he or she is gone. People come, people go. When they go, if you can manage it, give 'em a final, friendly pat on the ass. But don't waste time or tears watching the trailer slowly drive off into the sunset. "Auld Lang Syne" can be sung once a year. The rest of the time, it's "Next."

There is a proactive, protective measure I strongly suggest: avoid over-dependence on any one person – or, for that matter, thing – in any category of life but the one that could get you in trouble for polygamy. **In business, the worst number is one**. One key client, one major account, one employee in a vital role, one vendor, one media, one product, one income stream. The next worst number is two. If you are going to have an inside salesperson, at least cut the country in half and have two. Never let any one client, account, or distribution partner control more than twenty percent of your income. Beware, beware, beware lazy or over-confident or ignorant over-reliance on any one media, especially if that's online media. I explore this and related matters in great depth in my book *NO B.S. RUTHLESS MANAGEMENT OF PEOPLE AND PROFITS*. It's my most important and least popular book.

> **IN BUSINESS, THE WORST NUMBER IS ONE.**

Reading it is discomfiting, to say the least. Might save you a lot of grief. Might make you a lot of money.

Earlier, I said no one is irreplaceable, but I misspoke with regard to business. In your business, there is one irreplaceable person: you. Everyone else is dispensable, and they need to know it. At the same time, over time, you may very well want to return to the rule as first stated and deliberately make even yourself replaceable, so that the company of your creation can be passed to the next generation or sold, and can carry on without you.

18

DON'T WASTE YOUR MONEY ON IMAGE BUILDING ADVERTISING

(JOHN EDWARDS STILL THINKS HE'S A ROCK STAR.)

(Ben)

So, you think that mailing your newsletter once a month is good enough? Think that because you did a good job with a client he or she will actually remember you years (or even months) later? Will the client understand that "personal injury" [or name YOUR niche] means everything you think it means? Think again.

How many times have you had a former client for whom you did a great job say to you: "I didn't know you did that, too."

Shortly After the John Edwards criminal trial, I was trolling the TV. I can't even remember why I had the time. Maybe

Matt (12) and I were waiting to catch a few innings of the Nationals game.

The John Edwards jury was doing a road show. I hope you saw them, especially if you are a trial lawyer. Amazing to see what they were *still* looking for from the very experienced trial lawyers who tried the case. Amazing what they said about the complexity of the jury instructions. (Amazing, too, that some of them thought he was guilty, but not "that guilty.")

What I caught, though, was that at least one juror said that she had NEVER EVEN HEARD OF JOHN EDWARDS before trial began. Didn't know who he was!

How can that possibly be? The guy ran for vice president and he's been in the news almost ever since. He cheated on his dying wife. You'd have thought that this juror would have at least seen his face plastered on some tabloid somewhere.

Nope. Millions spent on the John Edwards "brand" – positive and negative. And it missed her!

Now go back to your own client and "fan" list. Ask yourself whether your message is staying in front of them enough. I'll bet that it's not. Does each and every monthly mailed newsletter tell your story, at least in some way? I am as guilty as anyone of assuming that they know my story. It's not good enough. That's why we are always ramping it up, direct mail-wise, at

BenGlassLaw. My graphic designer and I spent an hour planning out "what comes next." My question to you is: what have you done since last week to assure that your story is told over and over again? Of course, it must be told within the context of information you're giving to them, but it must be told. Don't be lazy about this.

WHAT HAVE YOU DONE... TO ASSURE THAT YOUR STORY IS TOLD OVER AND OVER AGAIN?

19 DON'T SHAKE ON IT

(Dan)

In my father's day, a handshake agreement was the order of the day and a pre-nup almost unheard of. Things change. It would be nice to be able to advise only doing business with people with whom you could settle for handshake agreements, but that would narrow the field a lot. After all, Diogenes went off in search of the completely honest man quite some time ago and, as far as I know, has never returned. Everybody I've ever worked with has some stupid reason why he or she doesn't need written documentation of deals with somebody – father, brother, college buddy, etc. – and they all wind up later shocked at getting screwed. Here it is, pure and simple: if you insist on conducting business in an un-businesslike manner without business correspondence and business documents, you deserve everything you get or don't get, and you forfeit right to complaint. Now here's a great story about the handshake agreement from Burt Reynolds:

A DEAL FOR LIFE

TransAm sales skyrocketed 700% after Smokey and the Bandit, and a Pontiac executive said, "You'll get a TransAm *for life.*" So I gave the first one to my sister, then I gave one to my brother, and I gave one to my co-star Jerry Reed. The fourth year, I didn't get one. I didn't want to be an asshole and say, "Where's my car?" But it wasn't there. So I called, and they said, "The guy who promised you that – he died."

Source: MAXIM Interview 2/08

20 DON'T LET YOUR CRITICS GET TO YOU

(Ben)

Do you listen to the noise that is said about you? Are you doing things in your market and your marketing that are disruptive enough to make people think about you, even if they don't like you? I see it from time to time. Someone will post something about me or GLM on some listserve and a member will forward it to me as sort of a "just letting you know what they are saying" note. I really appreciate it.

I do. We hang them up as "awards" in the office. One guy keeps writing me to tell me I'm wrong because the only "true" way to "market" is to try "honorable cases, even if they are dead losers, not write books, and optimize web sites." I think that's a recipe for a direct path to bankruptcy.

Stephen Covey (*7 Habits of Highly Effective People*) had critics. I learned that after reading several articles that followed his death. (At 79, he died of complications from a bicycling accident, which occurred when he lost control of his bike while coming down a hill pretty fast.)

You are likely familiar with Covey and his "7 Habits." Rem Jackson and I have covered the topic in the past on our Great Legal Marketing/Mindset monthly calls.

Did you know his story? He took on the "business leadership" establishment and its complicated and technical path to achievement written by highly paid "consultants" (think: *In Search of Excellence*) with his short, simple "principles." He talked a lot about self-reliance, personal responsibility, and self-improvement. There wasn't one magic blue pill for becoming an effective leader, but there were core principles.

After he became really interested in teaching leadership principles while participating on a mission trip for his church, he eventually started the Covey Leadership Center (later merging it with Franklin Quest to become FranklinCovey.) In a decade, it grew from a two-person company to seven hundred employees, with an annual revenue of seventy-five million dollars. Think about that: writing books, creating "day planners," giving speeches. Something, frankly, to be curious about and to use as a model.

Did you know he had detractors? According to the obituary that appeared in the *Washington Post,* some were critical that he was "capitalizing on the anxieties created by a fast-changing global economy" and that "he erred in placing all responsibility on the individual." Another (who happened, it turns out, to be a Karl Marx fan) said that he was "peddling banal truisms to ambitious but doomed middle managers who dream of becoming chief executives."

So what? Didn't seem to bother him much. He kept writing and producing. He lived his core values.

Here's the teaching point: when you have core values that guide your living, it is much easier to shrug off the critics. There will always be those who are jealous of your success, which, in most cases, *is* created by your own individual initiative, your willingness to keep learning, and your impulse to "take action." When you get criticized for your marketing, feel free to share it with us.

DON'T STEP IN THE DOGMA

(Dan)

Anyone who tells you there is Only One Way and he or she is The One who knows The Way and has The List of dogmatic, inviolate rules is – with the arguable exception of Moses – full of baloney if benign, or attempting to separate you from your money by discouraging analytical thought and free will if commercial, or attempting far worse if evil. These people are dangerous to you and quite possibly to themselves. Anytime you are confronted with somebody positioning himself or his ideas this way, run.

In the direct-response advertising world – just like everywhere else – experts like making up rules and then selling them as religion, and, frankly, people like being sold such religion, so the fault here lies as much with the gullible as with those who sell to them. It takes two to complete a con job. I wrote a book titled *Break ALL the Rules*, but I also put rules into a "Direct Marketing Diet" in my *No B.S. DIRECT Marketing for NON-Direct Marketing Businesses* book. Why the latter? Because people want such things. Anyway, one of the celebrated wizards of direct-response copywriting insists no headline should be longer than seven words. This is based on his experience with longer headlines, but it is not supported by everybody else's experience. Certainly not mine. Eight of my ten most successful and profitable ads and most of my sales letters producing a million dollars or more have longer headlines. Another guru in this field insisted his entire life that any direct-mail piece sent in anything but a plain, sneak-up envelope with no business identity or copy on its outside was stupid; his format was the only worthy format. While his can be the best choice, well over ninety percent of all the successful direct-mail pieces mailed – to the tune of hundreds of billions of dollars – are designed contrary to his rules. The fact is, direct-mail and direct-response advertising is situational; different strategies are best for different situations. As with just about everything else in life.

DIFFERENT STRATEGIES ARE BEST FOR DIFFERENT SITUATIONS.

Highly successful people in any field have three things in common, relevant to this subject: (1) they have a bag of tried and true tricks to choose from, (2) they choose the best ones for each situation, (3) they fight the tendency to get trapped into a narrow-minded, one way as the only way mindset about what they do. You can play eighteen holes with one club, but no pro does; there are woods, irons, putters. Different clubs for different situations. Spin put on the ball or not for different situations. I know that much and I don't golf. Absolutism is fairly easy to sell because, as Cavett Robert said, most folks are still walking around with umbilical cords in hand looking for the place to plug 'em in--but *you* don't want to be buying such nonsense. A chief cause of failure is lust for simple and easy solutions to complex and difficult problems and opportunities.

Al Gore's movie title *An Inconvenient Truth* was brilliant – although the film more science fiction than science. Truth is often inconvenient to premise. For example, in 2007, every Democratic candidate in the primaries echoed the idea – this an exact quote – that it is IMPOSSIBLE to get ahead in America without a college education (so we must give every child one for free). However, a quick look at the Forbes 400 list of richest Americans or at the owners of the Inc. 500 listed fastest growth businesses presents an inconvenient truth. And just for the record, THE richest entrepreneur, Bill Gates, is a college dropout. Objective, factual presentations about anything are rare, because every presenter has an agenda. And everyone already has his or her mind filled to the brim with premises accepted as facts, so non-facts bought as facts accumulate and consolidate into unshakable belief. More than any other reason, this is why there are, by ratio, so few ultra-rich people; few people force themselves to separate fact from fiction in order to think accurately, debate honestly, and develop decisions totally based on reality. This kind of analytical thinking is discouraged by every major religion (except, maybe, Buddhism), by both political parties, by every stockbroker and money manager, by everybody with any sort of personal agenda. I was raised Lutheran and, in catechism classes, placed nose to the wall in the corner and otherwise chastised constantly by the pastor for daring to ask questions – like how does anybody know it took exactly seven days since there weren't yet any calendars (like the one at the gas station with the hot girls on every page), were there?

One of the most difficult things to do in life is to train, condition, and discipline yourself to be an objective and rational thinker.

It is difficult because all of your upbringing, academic education, religious indoctrination, political indoctrination, peer influence, and media seek to shortcut, discourage and even demonize such analytical thinking. It is difficult because it makes you unpopular. It is difficult because it often puts you at odds with family, friends or co-workers. It is difficult because it takes time and effort, the collection and assimilation of information, careful fact-checking, weighing differing opinions. It is difficult because it does not offer easy peace of mind or simple conclusions.

One of the greatest achievements in life is to train, condition and discipline yourself to be an objective and rational thinker.

In any case, if you bet your Barbie money on others' dogma, you can be sure you will ultimately lose most of it. Dogmatic approaches may seem to work for short periods of time but fall apart over time or under pressure.

The sweetest sound to the casino industry comes from the lips of a rich mark, who says: "I've worked out a SYSTEM." There have been two gambling systems with absolute, simple rules figured out – of the tens of thousands experimented with and falsely proclaimed valid, since ancient Rome. One is an escalation of wager amount, doubling or by more complicated formula, losing bigger and bigger until you win, typically deployed on 50-50 chance bets like red or black at the roulette wheel. This system neutered very easily by casinos' imposing maximum bet limits. The other, card-counting against single deck blackjack by teams. Prevented by casinos by rule, "eye in sky" observing and quick ejection of offenders – and blackballing them at all casinos. It almost seems like the universe is run by a casino boss. Just about the time somebody figures out an iron-clad, works every time, simple set of rules, he steps in, makes one little malicious adjustment, and the whole thing goes to crap.

Ready for the real rules? Rule #1: You don't win playing by anybody else's rules or by using anybody else's playbook. Sorry, it's just not that easy or simple. If you intimately associate yourself with hundreds of from-scratch multi-millionaire entrepreneurs as I have, and very seriously study thousands more, you will arrive at the unpleasant realization that they aren't all working out of the same "little blue book" and that you can't just get your hands on a copy and quickly join their fraternity. Worse, you'll find each of them – while sharing some key commonalities with many of the others – has, over time, with some difficulty, assembled his or her own personal, private playbook containing philosophy, navigational system, strategies, skills, and more, that he or she relies on. That reveals what you must do for yourself. <u>Rule #2:</u> The darned game itself keeps changing. These top achievers are three things: situational, agile/adaptive, and always acquiring new information and ideas to integrate into their personal playbooks. That's why, backstage, Trump asked me which *three* books I was currently reading. It's why I couldn't give him a nifty answer – because, at the time, and at most times, I'm reading five or six with a dozen waiting in the queue. It's why I've written more than one book and in this book recommended some of those to you and in those, recommend still others. It's why ultra-successful people read, watch, listen, inspect, seek out certain associations, endlessly explore. It's why a multi-millionaire and seven-figure income entrepreneur chock full of knowledge and experience can be found seated as students at another seminar of mine after five, ten, even fifteen years of attending the previous ones. It's why you see entrepreneurs and professionals earning top incomes participating in mastermind groups, coaching programs, retaining consultants and advisors, and traveling to conferences *a lot.*

DON'T GO IT ALONE

(Dan)

Here comes a crass commercial message! You got this book from Ben Glass and he had his own crass commercial purpose in mind. Ben subscribes to the philosophical ideas I advance in my chapters and has been on "Planet Dan" for many years. He has tremendous expertise and successful experience in implementing the business and wealth strategies and practices described here, and is a serious, long-time student of mine. Ben has his own coaching and mastermind programs for lawyers. He deserves your consideration if you are an attorney and not yet a member of Great Legal Marketing. You need teachers, mentors, advisors, sounding boards, encouragers, and supporters. You need a constant stream of information and inspiration. You need connection and association. We all do.

For many reasons. It's a very complicated world. There's a lot of pressure, just to keep up. Entrepreneurial isolation is natural yet dangerous. Human beings need to be understood, appreciated, respected, and encouraged or they go mad. You can't really thrive with a volleyball on which you've drawn a smiley face as your compatriot.

Choice of association is, of course, critical. Permitting the toxic or ignorant or foolish or inexperienced to encircle you is harmful. We put all kinds of scary warnings on packages of cigarettes. Too bad people don't come with appropriate warnings tattooed on them. Save us all a lot of trouble. But the answer is not simple isolation. **Nor is isolation the same as independence. Being an independent thinker is profoundly valuable and admirable. Being an isolated thinker is lazy or fearful or arrogant and foolish.** If you are to prosper and thrive, you will find ways to surround yourself with and associate with people who stimulate you intellectually and inspire you to achieve. Such association will not occur by happy accident. You have to seek it, strategically create it, and even be cheerfully willing to pay for it or to have it facilitated for you.

BEING AN ISOLATED THINKER IS LAZY OR FEARFUL OR ARROGANT AND FOOLISH.

You also need people who can get things done for you or who can connect you with people who can get things done for you – who can be trusted, relied on, who are expert, and who are experienced, who are valuable. It's like the Kevin Bacon game: you are separated by no more than six people from whatever you need. So you need to be in association with smart and capable people who are, in turn, in association with smart and capable people, etc. Your own contacts are not enough. Other peoples' contacts' contacts' contacts often hold the golden keys you most need.

"DON'T THINK YOUR WORST DAYS ARE CRAPPY – THEY AREN'T"

(Ben)

I'm writing this note as I watch the sun come up over my hotel in San Francisco, where I have spent the better part of the weekend attending a directors' and board meeting for Love Without Boundaries. For those who don't know, LWB is an organization that my wife Sandi and I support and are active in. LWB provides care, compassion, and hope for China's orphans. The biggest challenge the organization faces today and that you hear all the time is that China is the "world's fastest growing economy." Probably true, but ninety-five percent of the country is still rural and very poor. China does have one of the world's fastest growing rates of birth defects and, while I'm no epidemiologist, most who do know relate the rise to industrial pollution.

A more "silent" problem that LWB helps fight is the issue of the rather profound damage that can occur to the human brain as a result of not only the lack of adequate nutrition (many babies born with cleft lip and palate are not adequately fed), but also as a result of the lack of the touch and love of another human being. We've seen the rather profound differences that can occur in our own adopted Chinese children. In fact, like someone who is first introduced to the "new learning" of marketing when you join GLM and wonder how you are ever going to get your arms wrapped around it, Sandi and I have spent the last two and a half years immersed in the new learning of the science of the brain as we learn a new way of parenting that is often entirely different than the styles and techniques we used with our five biological children.

So why write about this today? I think there are a couple of good reasons. First, I think I have *crappy* days sometimes. Sorry, Ben, nothing compares to waking up in a crib or a playroom in some rural part of China, hungry, and where it's 40 degrees inside because they can't afford to turn the heat on. Second, there is a definite methodology to learning and implementing new stuff. For Sandi and me, our first reaction when we hear some of what we need to change in our own lives is *you've got to be kidding; that makes **no sense** – these folks don't know about my kids.* By the time we've read the fourth scientific paper or book on a particular issue, however, "masterminded" with other parents who are a little further down the path than we are, and sought out advice and personal consultation from real experts, our thoughts and our behaviors change.

Sometimes we move two steps forward and one step back. That is the nature of learning and implementing new things. We don't give up. We don't go back to our old way of parenting. We do reach out to our support group and "mastermind." We do seek out and read and study even more. Finally, we seek inspiration from those loving parents who face even more difficult challenges than our crew provides.

It's also cool that sitting with me on the Board of Directors are (1) a physician who has built a huge dermatology practice that divorces its income from what insurance companies are willing to pay and rejects many industry norms in order to serve her lifestyle; (2) a financial planner who has built his business serving the ultra-successful; (3) a guy who left the corporate world to become a thought leader and consultant to businesses who are interested in building leaders within their organizations; (4) and a guy who is an international finance expert. The conversations in the hall are amazing.

By the way, this is a very worthy charity,
LoveWithoutBoundaries.com.

DON'T LISTEN TO JUST ANYBODY

(Dan)

Everybody's **eager** to dispense wisdom – the problem is the shortage of wise people.

Ordinary people, average Joes and Janes, have a kind of innate intelligence and common sense that seems vastly superior to a lot of so-called intelligentsia we observe from afar. Most New York cab drivers have more sense than most people in Congress or the academic theorists who too often surround a U.S. president in, sadly, the same way mystics once surrounded kings. Doubt it – just ask a cabbie how the country ought to be run. He'll tell you. And to be perfectly fair, we experts can sometimes grow arrogant, go beyond the scope of our true expertise in dispensing advice, or even know too much about why something won't work. There are also a lot of phony experts running around. There are a lot of fat doctors who smoke. In choosing an expert advisor or coach, by the way, there are three chief considerations: one, his or her relevant experience; two, the currency of their real world, successful, relevant experience; three, proof of positive results assisting others in your field or a comparable one.

The greatest danger to most people is the cabbie, not the (bona fide) expert. Far too many businesspeople are far too often influenced and far too easily subdued by people around them who are utterly unqualified to offer opinion, advice, or criticism about their plans or activities. Being utterly unqualified stops no one from meddling. Your employees, the guy in the shop down the street, your brother-in-law the auto mechanic, your spouse, heck, everybody has an opinion about your advertising – but how wealthy have they become with advertising? That's the "relevant experience thing." That brother-in-law may be the prefect guy to listen to about that odd little noise your buggy makes going uphill, but he's the last guy to listen to about your direct marketing campaign. Oh, and just because your sister's kid calls himself a website developer does not mean he knows anything about developing *content* for web sites *that sell*. In fact, it's a safe wager of your Barbie™ money that he doesn't. Beware, beware, beware.

Often, people eagerly sharing their opinions and dispensing free advice have their own agendas – consciously or unconsciously. It shouldn't surprise you; most of the people around you are not all that thrilled at seeing you far surpass them in success of any kind, but especially financially. You make them look bad. You call into question their brilliance. Their spouses may be inspired by you to ask them: if you're so damn smart, why aren't you rich? They may genuinely worry about being left behind. All sorts of inner issues can color their comments to you. Recall the cliché misery loves company. Misery is generally not very celebratory of others' success either. Beware, beware, beware.

The more ambition you exhibit, the more you visibly do, the more success you achieve, the more everyone around you will have lots of opinions about what you're doing wrong.

So who *should* you listen to most? Yourself. Famous super-attorney Gerry Spence talks about listening to his gut and his heart as he proceeds through opening statements, cross-examinations, closing arguments, and modifying his planned work on the fly. Mail-order maven Lillian Vernon spoke of relying on her "golden gut" in picking products for her hugely successful catalogs. Trump sees invisible potential for creating value in properties no one else sees, so much so that he points out he has *over-paid* for all his best acquisitions. I bring a lot to the **LISTEN TO YOUR GUT AND HEART** table in my work with my clients, but I also strive to work only with clients who themselves bring a lot to the table, so there can be collaboration. If you don't have a "golden gut" about your business, you're in for trouble. That's why being a super-serious student of everything about your business and your customers,

about human psychology and why people buy, about what I call "money math" – like that in my books *NO B.S. PRICE STRATEGY* and *NO B.S. RUTHLESS MANAGEMENT OF PEOPLE AND PROFITS,* about salesmanship and direct-response advertising as disciplines, are critical. If you aren't studying up every single day, you are failing at a prime responsibility. One of my key questions is: *what do you know at today's end about your business that you didn't know this morning?* You have no right to progress absent good answers to that question. Why should your income increase if your value isn't increasing?

Information is an essential foundation for insight and intuition. You can't have a "golden gut" without a whole lot of "golden information." This is also why it's important to participate in quality association, like organized mastermind groups and coaching programs, seminars, and workshops, one on one relationships with carefully chosen advisors, where you can not only acquire information but play out your ideas without having them attacked and destroyed at first sight. By the way, a really good teacher, coach, advisor does not just stuff information in – he draws your knowledge, insight and intuition out. *Educere,* the Latin root of *educate,* means "to lead out" – not to stuff in. Of course, that presumes there's value in there to be led out.

This is why it's called *SELF*-improvement.

There are lots of ways you can engage in SELF-*sabotage*. Just as, ultimately, all improvement is self-improvement, all sabotage is self-sabotage. If you don't do it to yourself, you at least permit it to be done to you. One form of self-sabotage is permitting excess influence by unqualified people. Another is to stop studying, intellectually atrophy, and be ill-equipped for your tasks, so that you can't trust yourself and grow evermore dependent on others and at risk to undue, unqualified influence. I'm in the advice-giving *business* and it's likely whoever brought this book to you is too. I am of best value to strong clients. I am not looking for dependence; I'm facilitating independence. That's the kind of advisor you want, and that's the kind of client you want to be.

"Don't squat with yer spurs on."

-Texas Bix Bender

AFTERWORD & NOTES

If you liked this little book, by all means, buy some – a dozen, a hundred, a thousand and give 'em out to customers, clients, friends. You can buy them in bulk as-is, customize them with your identity, or even be licensed to step in as a co-author for your own unique edition. For assistance, contact Pete Lillo at PeteThePrinter.com or 330-922-9833. If you didn't like the book, hush.

If you would like to know more about Dan's other works, visit DanKennedy.com and NoBSBooks.com. But do not send messages to him there by e-mail. These are publishers' sites, not his, and he does not use e-mail. Dan is available for a very limited number of interesting speaking, writing or consulting assignments, and you may communicate directly with his assistant, Vicky, about such matters via fax: 602-269-3113.

You can also find all his full-length books at amazon.com, via its Kindle®, and at bn.com, Barnes & Noble's online bookstore. Many but not all are also in stock at most bookstores.

Ben's books, CDs, DVDs, books and marketing toolkits are available at www.GLMWebStore.com. Use the code "barbie50" to get a $50.00 discount on orders over $150.00. You can find out more about Ben at www.BenGlassLaw.com and www.GreatLegalMarketing.com.

Both Dan and Ben consider themselves provocateurs. Our purpose is to make you think. Whether by annoying, offending, making you want to argue, or encouraging and inspiring, by sarcasm or straightforward talk, it doesn't matter—as long as we make you think.

WA